HERALDRY AND YOU

HERALDRY AND YOU

Modern Heraldic Usage in America

J. A. REYNOLDS

THOMAS NELSON & SONS

Edinburgh   NEW YORK   Toronto

DESIGN BY FRANK KARPELES

Library of Congress Catalog Card Number: 61-15047

MANUFACTURED IN THE UNITED STATES OF AMERICA

For my son
SHERMAN
who, despite his youth, has learned to enjoy the science of
heraldry as well as its brave forms and brilliant colors.

ACKNOWLEDGMENTS

Whatever is clear and coherent in these pages I owe to my wife and to our very good friend Hazel Gragg Sullivan (Mrs. Roy A. Sullivan). Though often resisted at the time, their suggestions, based on reading and rereading the various stages of the manuscript, have always resulted in greater clarity and conciseness.

Unfortunately, I cannot list separately the many individuals who have given me permission to display their armorial bearings in this work; their names, appearing under the arms, will have to express my thanks and gratitude. Some of them may be disappointed in a sense; for, whenever two or more branches of a family bore slightly different patterns of the same arms, I have generally used the basic form. This choice has allowed me to include a greater number and variety of arms.

I must express my deep appreciation for the help and cooperation shown me by Mr. George W. Rosner, Head of the Circulation Department in the University of Miami Library. And I must express as well my sincere gratitude to Mrs. G. T. Prior, Secretary and Editor of the South Carolina Historical Society; her assistance let me accomplish during a short visit to Charleston what might otherwise have taken weeks of correspondence to achieve.

Last, but highly significant, is the debt every modern writer owes to those three important members of the team: his publisher, his editor, and his production editor.

CONTENTS

	Introduction	13
I	Heraldry and You	17
II	You and Your Family Arms	21
III	Taking Your Coat-of-Arms Apart	51
IV	Using Your Coat-of-Arms	72
V	How Family Arms Grow	97
VI	Recording Your Arms	106
VII	Corporate Arms	111
VIII	The Symbols of Heraldry	119
	A Selected Bibliography	175
	Index of Blazons	177

List of Illustrations I

	Figure	Page
Component Parts of a Coat-of-Arms	69	51
Crest of the Chapel of the Venerable Bede	79	66
Divisions of the Shield and the Reference Points	72	53, 54
Double Quatrefoil, The	159	132
Fan-Crest, The	78	65
Flanches	182	145
Heraldic Tinctures and Furs	74	56
Label, The	190	152
Marshalling Arms	122	101
Partition Lines	202	159
"Plunckett" and Allied Arms, The	81	70, 71
Shield, The	70, 71	52

List of Illustrations II

Coats-of-Arms

	Figure	Page		Figure	Page
Aherne (1)	1	17	Bruce	157	132
Aherne (2)	163	135	Bryant, Rev. James C. Jr.	125	115
Anderson	2	17	Buck	141A	125
Barnwell	143	126	Bull	6	20
Barrett	136	122	Burke	167	137
Barry	135	122	Burns	7	22
Beck (1)	171	138	Butler	117	94
Beck (2)	130	120	Byron	139	124
Berkeley	207	165	Cameron	8	23
Blair	195	154	Campbell	188	148
Blake (1)	153	131	Carroll	175	142
Blake (2)	9	23	Carroll, Bishop Coleman F.	124	114
Boyd	152	130	Chamberlain	10	23
Briggs	3	18	Chaucer	11	23
Brindley	4	19	Chisholm	12	24
Brisbane	5	19	Clapp	217	170
Briscoe	165	135	Clark	13	24
Brodie	213	168	Clay	14	25

Coats-of-Arms

	Figure	Page		Figure	Page
Clery	15	25	Hawley	45	38
Clopton	141	124	Hay	176	143
Coffey (Coffee)	16	25	Hayne	199	157
Coffin	17	25	Heriot	158	132
Colleton	18	26	Heyward	46	39
Collins	19	26	Hillis	47	39
Colonna	20	27	Holbrook	170	138
Connolly	21	27	Hollingsworth	211	167
Corbett	22	28	Home	48	40
Costello	23	28	Homer	49	41
Crawford	24	28	Horner	50	41
Crosland (Crossland)	164	135	Houston	51	42
Cummings (Cummins)	25	28	Howard	138	124
Cunningham	201	158	Hutson	154	131
Cusack	200	157	Hynes	160	133
Dacre	26	29	Innes	52	43
Davenport	180	145	Izard	53	43
Davis	27	29	Jordan	54, 203	44, 159
Devereux	177	144	Kennedy (1)	55	44
Douglas	162	134	Kennedy (2)	189	149
Dowd	28	30	Kerr	56	44
Drake	212	168	Klaveness	57	45
Drummond	29	30	Lacy	58	45
Dundas	30	31	Latimer	183	146
Elliot	31	32	Launcelot, Sir	77	62
Erskine	198	157	Lee	142	125
Ferguson	32	32	Lindsay	59	46
Fitzgerald	33	33	Lippe	137	123
Fitzpatrick	168	137	Lockhart	150	129
Fleming	34	33	Logan (Maclennan)	60	47
Forbes	35	34	Loring	61	47
French	36	34	Louisiana State University	127	116
Gibbs	178	144	Lowy	62	48
Gilfoil (Gilfoyle)	37	35	Lucy	146	128
Gillentine	38	35	Lynch	63	48
Grady	120	100	MacDonogh (MacDonough)		
Gragg	187	148	(McDonogh)	155	131
Graham	209	166	Macewan	179	144
Grant	39	35	MacFarlane (MacFarlan)	64	49
Greby	40	35	Mackenzie	145	127
Hahn	41	36	Maclennan (Logan)	60	47
Halliday	42	36	Malcolm (McCallum)	65	49
Hamilton	43	37	Manners	66	49
Hannon	172	138	Manning (1)	75	57
Harleston	205	162	Manning (2)	67	50
Harrington	184	147	Martin	134	121
Hatfield	44	37	Matheson	68	50

Coats-of-Arms

	Figure	Page		Figure	Page
McArthur	161	134	Snooks (1) (Sennocks)	148	129
McCarthy	132	121	Snooks (2)	149	129
McGill University	128	116	Stackhouse	156	131
Meehan (Meighan)	82	72	Stafford	98	82
Menzies	83	73	Standish	99	82
Meriwether	194	154	Stanford	151	129
Middleton	185	147	Stokes	100	83
Morgan	84	73	Sullivan	76	61
Moultrie	214	169	Sutherland	101	83
Munro (Monroe)	85	74	Thompson	215	169
Murphy	186	147	Tierney	102	84
New Orleans, City of	216	170	Tobin	103	85
Noble	86	75	Tomkins (Tompkins)	169	138
Noble, John T.	70	52	Torrence (Torrance)	104	85
Nugent	87	75	Travis	105	86
O'Day	80	68	Tulane University	129	116
O'Toole	88	76	Tully	106	86
Percy	193	153	Turner	208	166
Plowden	89	77	United States of America		
Pollàtsek-Portos	73	55	(Arms of the Republic)	123	112
Power	90	77	Urquhart	107	87
Pratt	174	142	Vance	204	160
Price	91	78	Van Roy	191	153
Raleigh (1)	131	120	Visconti	218	172
Raleigh (2)	192	153	Waller	140	124
Reade	92	78	Walsh	144	127
Reynolds (1)	206	163	Washington	133	121
Reynolds (2)	118	95	Wayne	108	88
Reynolds II, Sherman Briggs	71	52	Welsh (Welch)	196	155
Rhett	93	79	Willard	109	89
Roach (Roche)	147	128	Willson	110	89
Rust	181	145	Woodward	111	90
Schrader	197	156	Woolridge	112	90
Scott	94	79	Wragg	113	91
Seabrook	95	80	Wright (1)	173	139
Seton (Seaton)	166	136	Wright (2)	114	92
Shakespeare	119	98	Yale University	126	116
Shelley	210	166	Yeamans (1)	115	93
Sherman	96	80	Yeamans (2)	116	93
Simons	97	81	Zomorano y Gonzalez	121	100

INTRODUCTION

I believe that until now every book in English currently in print and dealing with heraldry in a general sense is concerned primarily with the several systems in use in the British Isles. The bibliography in the back of this volume names several. They are excellent; but, by their nature, their interest is chiefly academic and peripheral for Americans.

A general book on heraldry to be of practical value to Americans must cover, understandably and with a minimum of technical language, two broad areas of reference:

First, the historic. Heraldry is at once a science, an art, and a set of social practices. The armigerous (arms-bearing) families will want to know the social status and implied assertions symbolized by a coat-of-arms as well as its range of functions and employment. They will want to know the component parts of a coat-of-arms, the relative importance of those parts, and the relationship those parts bear to one another. They will want to know how to decipher a coat-of-arms with especial reference reference to the divisions and tinctures (colors) of the shield and the charges or symbols which appear on that shield. They will want to know something of the artistic conventions that may largely determine the "emblazoning" or graphic depiction of the arms.

Second, a description of current practice. Heraldry has been used extensively in Europe for more than eight centuries; it has been used sporadically in Anglo-Saxon America for less than four—longer in Latin America. This book is an attempt to summarize current practice: to give a reasonably unbiased and objective account of heraldic phenomena as they exist in the United States in the mid-twentieth century. Enough patterns have become evident to make such generalizations significant. Their validity, of course, can be no greater than my range of data and capacity to synthesize.

The heraldry of the British Isles, especially that of Scotland and England, is the most rigidly systematized in all the world. (Irish heraldry is much more flexible.) In America we have been faced from the beginning with a curious paradox. Our heraldry, in its physical forms, derives predominantly from that of the British Isles; but for the most part we have chosen, almost from the beginning, to disregard most of the sacred cows of the British systems. We Americans are an independent-minded people: if we use heraldry, we'll use it in our own way—which should not be surprising; this is precisely what the English, Scots, and Irish have done with reference to each other and to the cognate developments on the Continent.

I do not pretend to tell my fellow Americans what we *should* do; I am content, within my limitations, to point out what in fact we are doing. But no observer can be completely objective; there is something of the moralist in each of us. However, when I express a perference of value or make a recommendation, and I do both, I always give a warning signal of subjectivity. It is then the reader's privilege to exercise his own judgment, which he will anyway.

Finally, I believe that every illustration of arms appearing in this book—governmental, institutional, commercial, or personal—has been or is presently in use by an American organization or by one or more American families.

HERALDRY AND YOU

HERALDRY AND YOU

This book is about heraldry and you. Directly and indirectly every man, woman, and child in America makes use of a surprising number of heraldic devices. Look at the back of a dollar bill and you will see a full-scale version of a coat-of-arms: the arms of the United States. If you are an American citizen, those arms are yours, and yours to display—proudly. There are many people in other parts of the world who would exercise this privilege if they had it, but they don't have it.

1   AHERNE (1)

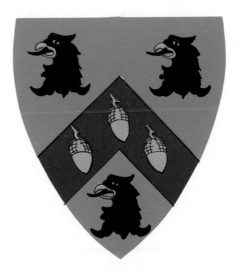

2   ANDERSON

Armory began as the special distinguishing mark of the fighting man. It still is. Every American soldier, sailor, airman, marine, or coast guardsman wears a specific heraldic device; when he doesn't, he is "out of uniform." He is entitled to display it in the full glory of its colors in his home. In a special form, it is worn or "displayed" (to use a technical term) by his wife, mother, sisters, children.

But arms are no longer (and haven't been for many centuries) limited to those in the Armed Services. Churches use them, both individual churches and entire communions. Just about every university, college, and high school in the land has its individual coat-of-arms to symbolize its corporate entity; and these arms become the heritage of the students—past, present, and future. Your Nation, your State, and most probably your community has a coat-of-arms, and each is yours to display.

Each club, society, or fraternal order to which you belong has provided

3   BRIGGS

you with a coat-of-arms that links you to it. The chances are that the automobile you drive displays a coat-of-arms. So possibly, does the brand of cigarettes you smoke. If you are a member of a professional association, a political organization, or an athletic club, the likelihood is that it has a coat-of-arms that is yours as its member.

As an American you probably have the undisputed "right" to enough coats-of-arms to fill an entire wall of your living room or den with a frieze of brilliantly colored shields.

Notice the trade-marks on the merchandise you buy; many of them are heraldic in nature or design.

18

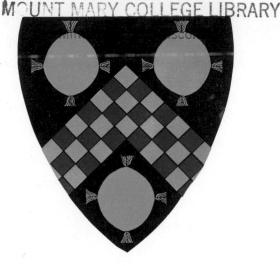

4   BRINDLEY   5   BRISBANE

Now much of this is "good" heraldry, which means that it accords in spirit
and practice with a long tradition of heraldic growth and usage. Much of it,
on the other hand, is made up of wistful and pitiful, mere hit-and-miss, at-
tempts at something barely understood, heraldically "illiterate." One purpose
of this book is to teach you to differentiate—to recognize at a glance the
sound, the traditional, and (I hope) the imaginative and creative as opposed
to the spurious, the merely hopeful, the imitative, or the cheap.

But all of these have been corporate arms. There are, however, several
millions of Americans who make use of family or personal arms. The number
is growing yearly; if it weren't, this book wouldn't be written. Are you one of
them? If so, where did you get your arms? Are they "living" or "dead" arms;
do you use them in some of the many and varied ways in which arms are
properly displayed, or are they merely a half-forgotten picture (possibly inherited from Aunt Jennie) on the living-room wall?

Do they grow with your family; do you know how to "marshal" them to
show family relationships? Are they something Aunt Jennie got from her Uncle
Maxwell? And, if so, how do they relate to *you?* Do you know how to "read"
them; or are they a mystery to you, like a framed page from a Sanskrit grammar hanging on your wall? Can you answer a question about them intelligibly;
or do you dread the question, armed against it only with the stock reply, "My
Aunt Jennie got them from her Uncle Maxwell; she always said they are the
Cuthbert arms"? And here you point for triumphant confirmation to the name
"Cuthbert" in Old English lettering about an inch and a half below the somewhat faded but still colorful representation in oils. Incidentally, your own
maiden name is Anderson and your husband is a Plunckett.

19

Who is entitled to a coat-of-arms? What is its status? What coat-of-arms should you use? In how many ways can you use such heraldic devices with propriety and in good taste? Where and how do you go about getting them recorded, registered, or matriculated? And how much does it cost?

How do you use coat armor with confidence? If you want to know, this book is about heraldry and for you.

6   BULL

YOU AND YOUR
FAMILY'S ARMS

What They Say About You

The moment you claim and use your family coat-of-arms in any way you automatically make an assertion about yourself. Just what that assertion is depends on the historic implications of coat armor and your willingness to meet the responsibilities that such use implies. To put it as briefly as possible, the assertion that a coat-of-arms makes is dual:

First, it asserts an identification. It identifies you not merely as an individual but as a member of a family, sept, or clan. If a coat-of-arms were meant to identify you solely and completely as an individual, unrelated to anyone else, then a serial number would serve just as well, probably better. Within reasonable limits (there are a few miscreants hanging from every family tree), presumably you are proud of your family, its struggles, its successes; its present, past, and possible future position. You bear your arms as you bear your name, not only for particularized identification (the serial number would do better), but also to establish a relationship with others who bear those arms or name. If you are not proud of the relationship, there is no law that says you must bear those arms; furthermore, the courts are generally ready to relieve you of the onus of the name as well. And, as you will see later in the discussion of "How Family Arms Grow" (Chapter V), a coat-of-arms is a symbolic language that can say much in little space; it can tell instantly your relationship to other families in a way that no "name system" could accomplish without using half a dozen or more compound forms. In bearing a coat-of-arms you become an avowed representative of the one or several families represented on those arms. And this leads naturally to the concomitant second assertion that you make when you bear arms.

For in the second place the display of arms is a forthright and confident assertion of status. Here the old expression *noblesse oblige* is particularly apt, for it was historically used to describe just this status; and it means simply that any rank or position that you inherit, assert for yourself, or accept, carries with it the obligation to meet its responsibilities with integrity, courage, and

7   BURNS

honor. In the area of social life, where family arms have no near competitor, these bearings are an avowal that you strive within your physical resources and your spiritual capacity to "live like a gentleman" and that you expect to be considered one. They are not an indication of great wealth, nor pretention, nor even (in the case of new arms) of "old family," nor for that matter of a high level of educational or cultural attainment; but they are a sign of gentility. To put it most succinctly, if you are a product of and exemplify gentle birth or breeding, or if you have achieved it in yourself, you are entitled both morally and in the technical sense to the use of arms. That is still the basis for the "granting" of arms in every country where arms are regulated by law. They are an open recognition of your status as a lady or gentleman.

To understand why these two implications of arms bearing are true, it is necessary to know how and among whom the custom of using these symbols arose and how they reached their present somewhat divergent status in different cultures.

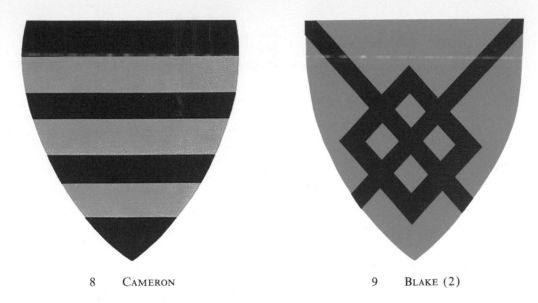

8   CAMERON   9   BLAKE (2)

Their Origins and Early Use

From the very beginning, a coat-of-arms served as a ready and crucially necessary—in fact, a life-and-death—means of identification, especially in the pell-mell and confusion of a Donnybrook.

The fighting man of the Middle Ages wore such armor as he could scrape together. The more fortunate wore a shirt of chain mail, with or without long sleeves, and coming as far down to protect as much of his body as his resources or resourcefulness provided. He wore one or another shaped head covering, preferably of metal. Both of these were supplemented, inside or outside, by padding. His shield or buckler went through a variety of shapes and sizes; though it was generally made of tough wood, covered over with some sort of hide and reinforced by metal strips. Over his body armor he wore a long sur-

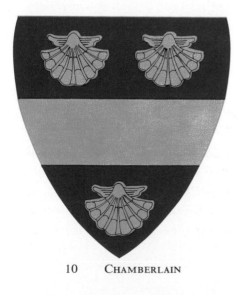 

10   CHAMBERLAIN   23   11   CHAUCER

coat of cloth (rough homespun wool, linen, or silk—costly as his purse could bear) and girdled at the waist by his sword belt. This surcoat too was probably padded as an added protection. Some, unable to afford metallic body armor, wore only this surcoat with heavy padding beneath it. It is customary to say, as we increasingly view the Middle Ages with romantic eyes and focus only on the wealthy knight with his sometimes almost inhibiting heavy metallic armor, that this surcoat was worn *primarily* to protect the metal, highly susceptible to rust, from rain and fog and dew. This is to ignore the realities of the time; for many a fighting man the heavily padded surcoat was his only protective body armor—until or unless, having survived a day of fighting, he could scavenger more durable pieces at dusk from some fallen foe or friend. And there is still another and perhaps more cogent reason why even the fight-

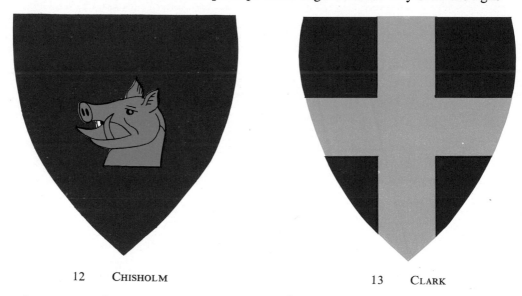

12   CHISHOLM   13   CLARK

ing man equipped with chain mail would want to wear a surcoat—precisely to disguise the fact. He could thus hide his advantage and encourage combat on the part of an adversary who wore only padding, just as the U.S.S. *Kearsage* hid her metallic armor behind a wooden hull when seeking battle with the unarmored C.S.S. *Alabama*.

So attired in padding, surcoat, and helmet, and carrying a shield, the fighting man, whether knight or foot soldier, was not easily recognizable in the heat of a fray. It became customary then for members of a single family, group, sept, or clan to emblazon—probably at first with crude daubs of paint—some identifying sign or symbol on the surcoat—front and back. This became a uniform identification for members of the group. This device, one large symbol or several repeated smaller ones as fancy dictated, was soon extended in its

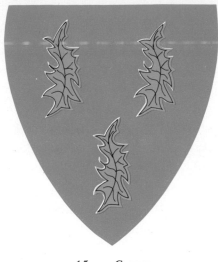

14   CLAY   15   CLERY

use to other items of standard equipment; it was painted boldly on the padded horse blankets of the mounted soldiers, on the shields of all members of the unit, and even on the head coverings. Its appearance on morion, helmet, or cap did not yet betoken what we now call the crest; it was merely a meaningful repetition of the identifying symbol wherever it could be seen.

The tradition of highly disciplined teamwork that was so characteristic of the armies of classical Rome had been dead for centuries. This one new discovery of the identifying and linking symbolic device made highly organized warfare possible in the Middle Ages; the Crusades could not have been fought without it. Until the development of missiles propelled by gunpowder, this armorial bearing was a military development second in importance only to the invention of the stirrup.

In studying the history of coat armor we have let ourselves focus attention

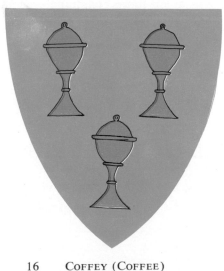

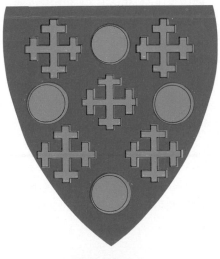

16   COFFEY (COFFEE)   25   17   COFFIN

too exclusively on the company commander or knight; we have been understandably swayed by the glamour of rank and position. Because he wore such bearings, the commanding officer linked himself to his men; but because they wore identical symbols they linked themselves to him and to each other.

This identifying surcoat—the original "coat-of-arms"—was so important that it has given its name to all armorial bearings that grew out of it. For several centuries now the depiction of an armorial achievement has normally displayed a veritable array of military accoutrements—except one: and that, perhaps not incuriously, is the original coat-of-arms, the surcoat. The fanciful and "artfully ragged" mantling so often depicted in armorial achievements is not a pictorial representation of the surcoat. It will be discussed in the next chapter.

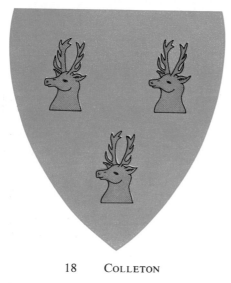

18   COLLETON

19   COLLINS

Medieval feudal life—except in the towns and cities, which were by their nature a negation of the feudal system—was much more communal and inbred than the more sophisticated and highly individualized modern cares to admit. The feudal estate, when feudalism was at all functional, was largely a self-supporting and interlocking community, a web of interdependence. Precisely as aboard a modern fighting ship, every able-bodied man has at least two primary responsibilities (not to mention collateral duties); he had his housekeeping duties, whether to till the soil, work in or manage the mill, the smithy, or manage the accounts; and he had his battle station. These men owed battle service to their lord, perhaps a vavasor, just as he in turn owed similar service to his lord, and he to his. Feudal life was based on a continuous and presumably indissoluble chain of command. Technically speaking, there was no "ownership" of land from most elevated noble to humblest tiller of the soil (and, in England, there hadn't been since the coming of the Normans); certain people merely "held" land from someone else and, in turn, sublet it to others. Ultimate ownership resided in the crown, as represented by the sovereign. Theoretically at least, each man in the chain held his land for the benefit of those who shared it with him. (This concept, unfortunately, was more honored in the breach than the observance.) And under such a system the basic unit was the agricultural feudal community, the manorial estate.

When the fighting was over and the survivors returned to the community, often bringing with them for the widows and children the accoutrements of those who did not return, the same scene was repeated in each dwelling. The lord of the land, whether franklin, knight, or great noble, proudly displayed his shield and other arms in manor house, hall, or castle; the independent yeoman and humbler retainers hung theirs in cottage or hovel, as the case might be; but, if they had fought together, the markings on every one of those shields were basically the same.

Even the stranger could be taken "under the protection of the lord," that is, adopted into the community, where he would probably marry and his children would become an even more integral part of it.

In times of peace, the lord of the land or one or more of his sons would bear those arms—and bear them more resplendently than they ever appeared in battle—into the lists of formal tournaments and jousts. He and his wife, his sons, and daughters, would wear them richly embroidered on their clothes to the elaborate and formal social gatherings of the day; for formality, order, and decorum were the characteristics of the age. He and all his family bore them

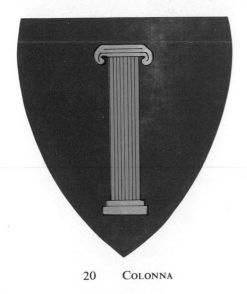

20   COLONNA

21   CONNOLLY

22   CORBETT

23   COSTELLO

proudly on those rare state occasions of an appearance at court. In death they graced his bier and proclaimed his identity even from the tomb.

But there were numerous occasions in peacetime when the humbler members of the community carried their arms, and necessarily displayed the armorial devices recorded on them. They wore them defensively when traveling with their families to the great fairs and to the smaller ones nearby; they wore them as formal attire in the processions of the great saints' days; they wore them to participate in those elaborate drills and mock battles (the poor man's tournaments) associated with the Hock Tuesday plays, the sword dances, the St. George's plays, the Robin Hood pageants, and the general May Day celebrations.

24   CRAWFORD

25   CUMMINGS (CUMMINS)

Then came the decline of feudalism and that long period of transition in which ownership of land in the modern sense was developed. With jealous ownership of the land came jealous ownership of the arms; and the new "landlord" as opposed to the old "lord of the land" claimed both. So completely enmeshed were the concepts of land and arms that this confusion became the basic issue of the Scrope-Grosvenor trial (A.D. 1390). This was the most precedent-making, and perhaps the most famous, of all law cases involving the use of armorial bearings. Briefly, a family bought land and claimed the arms of the seller as inherent in the land. The result of that case was the ruling that arms are inherent in descent, not in a particular piece of land. Implicit in the case and its sequelae, however, was the concept that the ownership of land implied the right to arms, with the assumption that if the purchaser lacked arms he could apply for them as a grant from the sovereign. Such application was unnecessary in the case cited; the purchaser had arms in his own family and merely continued to use them.

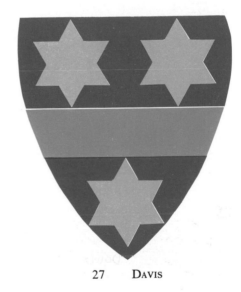

26   DACRE   27   DAVIS

But the old cohesion of the feudal community had already been destroyed, at least in England. In Scotland and Ireland, however, the relationship (largely in reality, but partly on an adoptive basis) was transferred to blood, that is, a family or clan relationship, and continued much longer.

With the new social situation, the "right" to arms became increasingly associated with the ownership of land and its attendant social position. Arms became the distinguishing mark of the gentility, the hereditary landowners; the possession of arms set aside the "gentle" from the "simple." The right to bear them conferred privileges that equaled or surpassed those earlier educational advantages that entitled their possessor to claim "benefit of clergy." This phrase has become so restricted in modern usage that it now means little more than a religious marriage ceremony; but in the Middle Ages it had a broader area of reference implying privileges inherent in the clerical or "churchly" status, not the least of which was the right to trial by the canonical or church courts in preference to being hailed before the king's bench. As late as the Renaissance this right was being sporadically exercised: Ben Jonson claimed "benefit of clergy," basing his claim on the ancient accepted test—he could read and write Latin.

But the Scots and the Irish, with their strong sense of blood relationship as the basis of the clan, never popularly accepted this newer philosophy, though it was official and defended by those most likely to benefit from it. The Celtic clansman persisted in regarding the clan and its regalia as essentially his own.

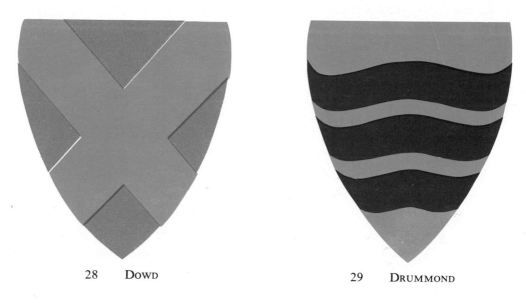

28   DOWD   29   DRUMMOND

The American Concept of Armorial Use

And it is precisely this family, clan, name relationship that has dominated the use of armorial insignia in what is now the United States. This has been true from the beginning.

Those of our early settlers who came from the British Isles—and they tended to dominate the social picture for the nation as a whole—were largely from north of the Humber, from Scotland, and from northern Ireland. Our population has been reinforced by many elements; but where there is a concept of armorial usage the basic pattern has not changed, except for those few who have been overawed by and wished to align themselves with official usage in England. Arms to the American are "family arms," reasonably shared by all.

30   DUNDAS

Arms and Gentility

In the centuries that followed the decline of feudalism, the concept of "gentry" and "gentility" underwent changes as well. Because these changes took the form of an orderly growth, the various countries of the British Isles were spared those excesses of social revolution that took place elsewhere.

Originally the term gentility referred to the gentle, that is, "known" or "recorded" families, the landowners. The word gentleman was a technical term; the man who bore this designation might be saint or scoundrel, but he was a gentleman if he was a member of such a family. But inherent in the code of chivalry was the doctrine of *noblesse oblige*. In terms of this doctrine and in accord with the code of chivalry, certain behavior patterns were expected of "gentlemen" and their "ladies." That such behavior was not always forthcoming was regrettable. The disappointment, instead of weakening the expectation, actually heightened it into a demand, a demand associated in extreme cases with the social ultimatum of ostracism; that is, the gentleman-by-blood who did not live reasonably within the behavior patterns of the gentleman-by-code was declared "no gentleman." This does not mean that he stepped gracefully

31

31   Elliot   32   Ferguson

into another acceptable social classification; the pariah has no place in any acceptable class. In days of greater social stability, when families lived for generations close to the land and in a given area, such a threat of ostracism was a most powerful social force.

At this point the concepts of gentleman-by-blood and gentleman-by-behavior supplement each other to provide a reasonable guarantee of both potential and performance. The first without the second guarantees nothing but a predatory class of landlords. The other extreme, a concept of gentility based solely on the criterion of gentleman-by-behavior was little better. No individual is an island; he inherits potentials for capacity and lack of it from all his stock. Even when the estimate of gentleman-by-behavior is accurate, it guarantees nothing beyond a single individual in a single generation; there is no opportunity for even a crude statistical estimate. This unilateral basis of gentility reached its peak in the expanding romanticism of the nineteenth century. It may be significant and in response to the umbrageous twilight of an easy egalitarianism that is was during that particular century that the use of coat armor reached its lowest level. It has since recovered.

But to those who continued to bear arms, the "check and balance" inherent in the dual concept of gentility still offered the best prospect for social, family, and individual responsibility. And this is the precise avowal and promise of the armigerous family, for this is what gentility still means in the bearing of arms.

The English System of Armorial Use

The historic concept of armorial usage in the United States has been to regard all branches of a related family bearing the family name as sharing equally and freely in the use of the undifferenced basic arms of that family. This is historically the general picture, though there have always been the few who chose to adopt the preciosity of more rigid foreign systems.

The American system, if the word is properly applicable, is certainly the loosest of all. If only to understand better what our own usage is, we ought to review very briefly some contrasting system. The most profitable to review for this purpose is that of England, and for these reasons: (1) The English system is official and highly codified. (2) In its philosophy and rigidity, it offers the greatest contrast. (3) It is the most articulate; most books and articles available to Americans are based on it. (4) In the past half-century it has influenced American usage more than any other system.

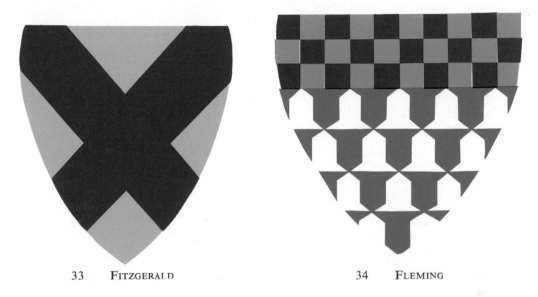

33   Fitzgerald   34   Fleming

The basic point of difference is in the philosophy of usage. Where American usage regards a coat-of-arms as essentially a "family badge," the official English viewpoint may be best expressed as "one man, one coat-of-arms," that is, theoretically no two living men should bear the same coat-of-arms. This is necessarily based on the legal concept of inheritance by primogeniture, that is, inheritance passing from eldest son to eldest son (or next in line). But primogeniture has never had significant roots in American soil.

Such a system, one man, one coat-of-arms, becomes complicated from the very outset; to be consistent, it requires an elaborate set of *cadence marks*[1] (minor additions to the father's arms) to differentiate the sons of even a single individual. (I say the *sons* because even this system has never attempted to

[1] All technical terms appearing in italics in this discussion are explained in the alphabetical glossary in Chapter VIII, "The Symbols of Heraldry."

"differentiate" the daughters.) Furthermore, the system can defeat itself in the next generation of a man who holds the original grant of a coat-of-arms.

Let us assume that a man receives a grant of arms consisting of a silver shield on which is pictured a blue elephant's head. Now he and he alone has the right to bear these arms on a shield in just this form, though his wife and daughters may display them, not on a shield, but on a *lozenge*. Even his sons do not have the legal right to display the same arms, but must *difference* them by cadence marks to indicate that they are not the legal owners of such arms. And special cadence marks have been assigned up to the ninth son. For instance, the eldest son adds a *label* (a sort of rakelike figure, usually shown with three short tines), and the second son adds a *crescent* (a figure of the crescent moon, pointing upward). These marks are normally placed in the upper-central part of the shield and cover anything that happens to be there.

Now if, in the lifetime of the father, these sons have children, then the grandsons are expected to add these same difference marks on top of the ones already there. The arms of the man's granddaughters and daughters-in-law, however, are still indistinguishable for the most part. When the grandfather dies, certain armorial changes must now take place: the eldest son now removes his label, for he has inherited his father's arms; simultaneously, his several children must now remove his label from their arms, but retain their own cadence marks which were previously placed on his label. However, the second son of the grandfather still retains his crescent; and his arms, bearing the crescent, now become the basic arms of his branch of the family. The system has already (at least from the American viewpoint) gotten itself rather complicated. To make matters worse, this second son of the grandfather now

35   FORBES   36   FRENCH

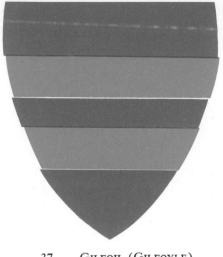

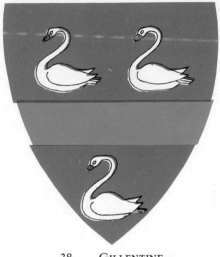

37   GILFOIL (GILFOYLE)   38   GILLENTINE

has arms identical with those of his nephew; that is, the second son of his elder brother. But the system *can* be made to take care of this contingency also; he and his nephew can color their crescents differently! However, in another generation or two, this system of in-family differentiation by cadence marks can become so complicated as to defeat its own purpose.

If I seem to imply some doubt as to the acceptability of this system to the American scene, the implication is neither wholly brash nor wholly American. One of the most conservative and comprehensive heraldic writers of modern times, the distinguished A. C. Fox-Davies, seemed to be equally dubious. He refers to this system of difference marks as "not a very important matter."[1]

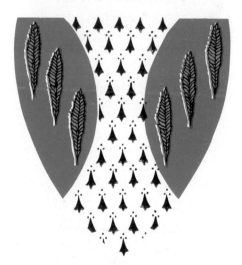

39   GRANT   40   GREBY

[1]Fox-Davies, A. C., *The Complete Guide to Heraldry*, Edinburgh, London, New York, Thomas Nelson and Sons, 1901, page 24.

But any dedicated system always has at least one alternate plan. If and when the system of differencing by cadence marks becomes too unwieldy, complicated, or otherwise unsatisfactory to a given family, its members then have recourse to another system of differencing, by making slight but basic changes to the coat-of-arms itself. Under English law, this requires re-matriculation or official cognizance. In developing this second system, the original changes may be very slight; for instance, the original elephant's head may have been *couped* (finished off at the bottom by a straight line). Now some branch of the family may carry the elephant's head *erased* (finished off at the bottom with a stylized form of three jagged points instead of by a straight line). Another branch may change the color of the tusks; still others may change the color of the head itself. Others may reverse the color and the metal, or change the metal from silver to gold, or from metal to one of the heraldic furs. Still others may divide the shield so that it is parti-colored, or the elephant's head may be metamorphosed into the whole animal; or the single head may suddenly proliferate into three or four, and some of these branches may place the collection of heads around a cross or other *charge*.

41   HAHN   42   HALLIDAY

This latter is certainly a more flexible system than the other, but from the American viewpoint it, too, has its weaknesses. Those weaknesses still grow out of the basic philosophy, "one man, one coat-of-arms." Carrying out this system consistently, the Scylla and Charybdis become obvious: on the one hand the changes may represent such minutiae as to be merely academic rather than practical; on the other, they may become so drastic as to obscure relationship.

43   Hamilton

The American would regard as a basic objection the fact that the unit of relationship indicated by the resulting forms is too limited. It can never extend significantly beyond one man and his immediate family; there is no coverage for our "kissing cousins."

Its one merit seems to be that it provides almost continuous work for the heralds. Few families have the know-how to make these continuous changes, and I suspect that even in England not every family is willing to co-operate to the extent necessary to maintain such an elaborate and complicated system at its meaningful best.

Current American Practice

Nevertheless, within the last half century particularly, this latter English system of differencing has had some very real influence on arms as borne in America.

44   Hatfield

The opposite is true of the Scottish system of differencing. The present Scottish system is based primarily on the use of *bordures* surrounding the basic arms. These bordures have various types of edges, internal divisions, and coloration. But, so far, the bordure system has had no impact on our American armory, and for that reason I am not discussing it here in detail.

In stating that the English system of differencing arms has made some headway in the United States, I am not talking about the marshaling of arms (discussed in Chapter V, "How Family Arms Grow"); I am speaking rather of slight though significant changes in the basic arms themselves. These changes follow the general pattern that I discussed in terms of English arms; however, they are broader in scope of use—so as to include our beloved kissing cousins —and somewhat geographical in nature.

45   HAWLEY

The pattern can best be stated in terms of an example. Several related branches that acknowledge each other of a given family live in the Alabama-Georgia area. The original region of settlement was in the Carolina-Virginia area. The Alabama-Georgia related units are aware of each other but over a period of generations have lost contact with those in the original area of settlement. Still, the family arms used by the several units of the transplanted Alabama-Georgia branch, perhaps copied diligently and by rote from a painting or from an engraving on family silver once owned by a common great-grandfather, is the same as that used by the Carolina-Virginia units. Somewhere along the line, and probably within the past fifty years, someone in the Alabama-Georgia group may have made some basic but slight change in the original arms to set themselves apart from other groups with whom they no longer have contact. The units in this area are in reasonably close touch with each other, and the new form of the arms is copied and spreads rapidly among most or all of them. The arms are still recognizably those of the larger clan but have an immediate local application to specific and more closely related

46   HEYWARD

units living, for the most part, within a limited geographical area. Other branches of the original family, now living severally in Texas, Missouri, and Illinois, may continue to use the original arms, or they, too, may have made (without reference to any of the other branches) changes of their own.

47   HILLIS

"Mrs. Plunckett" and her "Cuthbert" Arms

The situation discussed so far deals with a family in its various branches all of whom are descended from a common arms-bearing line and all of whom share the same name. The differences in the arms that one or more particular branches made, or may make, are normally trifling; they set apart a particular sept without disturbing the ability of those arms to indicate the basic relationship to the larger unit. Furthermore, within even the strictest sense of American usage, there is no doubt as to the right of all these people to the use of the basic arms of the family, differenced or undifferenced, as they choose.

48   HOME

The problem of "senior" lines of descent—so closely associated with the system of primogeniture and consequently highly significant in British heraldry —rarely, if ever, enters into the picture of American usage.

It is now time to pick up the thread of an almost facetious reference made in the preceding chapter: the case of "Mrs. Plunckett, née Anderson," who displays on her living-room wall a well-framed and excellent representation in oils of the "Cuthbert arms." This painting was given to her by her Aunt Jennie, a "Cuthbert," by the way, who in turn had inherited it along with a number of other family items and keepsakes from her paternal uncle, "Maxwell Cuthbert."

The case is fictitious but not hypothetical. It parallels at least half a score of similar cases of which I have firsthand knowledge. Every aspect of it deals with occurrences in reality in American heraldic usage, but every effort has been

49   HOMER

made to insure the anonymity of the real but unrelated cases out of which this fictitious case grows.

Amy Plunckett's general position and background need some broad explication to establish the situation. She lives on the Eastern seaboard in an old but small city that has been for more than two centuries the center of a predominantly agricultural area. The Pluncketts are not wealthy; but, along with various friends and neighbors (some much wealthier and some not so well off), they enjoy a social position and conserve a way of life that is highly respected in their community. This position is one they justify and exemplify in themselves and one which they have inherited from their forebears. Though Mrs. Plunckett might not care to admit it openly, there is a reasonable suspicion that the arms hanging on her wall are more than a décor or an heirloom; they are in all probability a symbolic assertion of a tradition that she preserves in herself and which her husband shares, and one which both of them are making a conscious effort to pass on in its best aspects to their children.

50   HORNER

The Cuthberts were among the original settlers in that region. A maiden cousin of Mrs. Plunckett's mother still has the original land grant, now carefully framed and sealed under glass. Even before our War of Independence, in which several of her ancesters distinguished themselves at least locally, the Cuthberts were (to put it modestly) among the well-known families of the county. In all modesty, however, Mrs. Plunckett would be the first to assure her close friends that "there are Cuthberts and Cuthberts" in that neck of the woods. She isn't especially proud of all the members of the clan; still, it is equally obvious that she is happy to belong to a branch that has, in good times and bad, rich or poor, been ever mindful of its civic and social responsibilities.

51   HOUSTON

Her grandfather was Jonas Cuthbert, the father of a fairly large family. His bachelor brother was Uncle Maxwell. One daughter was Mrs. Plunckett's mother; another was her Aunt Jennie. One son was Randolph Cuthbert, Mrs. Plunckett's uncle; and he, in turn, had one son, Edgar Jonas Cuthbert. Edgar, though his gallantry would never let him admit it, is the same age as his cousin, Amy Plunckett. They grew up together; both are married, and they have children of roughly matching ages. Edgar lives in a house not unlike his cousin Amy's and less than a block away. Their children go to the same schools and maintain a close relationship, as do their parents.

Among her other treasured heirlooms, Amy Plunckett has "a very fine painting" of her grandfather, Jonas Cuthbert. (It really isn't a very fine painting at all, but everybody in town says it is.)

When Edgar Cuthbert married (his wife, by the way, is not a local girl), they received from the family among their wedding presents a silver teapot

42

and several spoons, all of which were engraved with the Cuthbert arms. Several years later, Edgar's wife borrowed Mrs. Plunckett's framed picture of the Cuthbert arms and had a copy of it made. It is true, of course, that a competent heraldic artist could have produced such a representation from the engraving on the teapot or even from the spoons, but the local lady who did the job would not have been able to meet this challenge.

52   INNES

Almost immediately, Edgar's wife, who had been reared in a much more sophisticated community, began to make, not ostentatious, but reasonably free use of the Cuthbert arms. (Chapter IV, "Using Your Coat-of-Arms" will list some of these ways.) Furthermore, in recent years, other people that Amy knew began to make a somewhat freer use of armorial bearings than she could remember as having been general in her own youth. Mrs. Plunckett, always a conscientious woman, began to be dubious of her "right" to have the Cuthbert arms hanging on her wall; previously she had always regarded them in much the same light as she did her grandfather's picture.

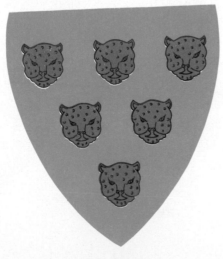

As time went on, a number of questions—some clear cut, others largely amorphous—developed in her mind. At the risk of doing Amy Plunckett's character an injustice, let's try to define some of those questions for her and then, still within the framework of current American heraldic usage, try to answer them.

(1) The first question is one that she had in fact already asked herself: Is it at all proper for me to have this painting of the Cuthbert arms hanging on my wall?

54   JORDAN

This is an easy one to answer. Yes, Mrs. Plunckett, you have every right to so display them. They are fully identified as being the Cuthbert arms, are so labeled, and they make no pretentions of being either Plunckett or Anderson arms. I notice that the facsimile of your picture of the Cuthbert arms that Edgar and his wife display is also labeled with the name. In their case this is totally unnecessary, but the practice is most common.

55   KENNEDY (1)

56   KERR

44

57   KLAVENESS

As a matter of fact, you have a legal right to put anything on your walls, especially if properly labeled. You might, if you wished, hang up the arms of the King of Siam; or, more appropriately, as an American you might show the arms of George Washington, which are presently used, incidentally, as the arms and the flag of the District of Columbia. Where propriety is concerned, however, the display on your walls of any family coat-of-arms, even if properly labeled, carries with it an assumption of relationship. In the case of the Cuthbert arms in your own household, this assumption is justified; in the case of some other set of arms, it might not be. There is no more reason why you shouldn't show your grandfather's arms, properly labeled, than his painting. If you still have qualms, you might—wall space permitting—hang both in the same panel, with the arms immediately below his painting.

(2) The second question that Mrs. Plunckett might conceivably ask is: Have I the right to make any other or more extensive use of the Cuthbert arms, such as my cousin Edgar and his wife do? After all, I *am* a Cuthbert; Edgar's wife isn't.

58   LACY

Here, Mrs. Plunckett, the answer is equally easy; but, from your point of view, not so satisfactory. I am aware of the fact that quite a few people in America do make fairly extensive use of arms from the maternal lines, but best usage does not condone it. As you imply, the situation that confronted you may seem unfair; it seems even more unfair, when we examine all the facts carefully, than your question and its attendant comment implied. As you know, I have gone over your genealogical data with you; and we are both aware, even within the limited extent that we have examined that genealogy, that you represent not one, but four lines of descent from the Cuthberts. One of those lines is through the Andersons, your father's family. It is true that your cousin Edgar's wife is not by descent a Cuthbert at all; what may seem even stranger to you is that your cousin Edgar himself (so far as I know) is a

59   LINDSAY

Cuthbert by three lines of descent, in common with you, and as compared with your own four lines. The mathematics of the case, while interesting in this instance, are not determining; the fact remains that in best usage we do not carry or make free use of unquartered maternal arms. So closely are arms associated with name, that is, with paternal descent, that in Scotland if you wished to carry your mother's arms you would be required to carry her maiden name also, foregoing your paternal name. As to Edgar's wife, the moment she married him and was so accepted as his wife, she shared with him his status, his name, and his arms. Parenthetically, we both know that she has her own paternal arms; and, despite the sanctions of current American usage, she has failed to take adequate advantage of them—either for herself or for her children. But this is a matter that will be discussed in Chapter V, "How Family Arms Grow."

(3) The third question, a logical outgrowth of the previous one, might be: Have I the right to use arms at all?

Mrs. Plunckett, by every conceivable standard—not only in the United States, but elsewhere—you have every right to the use of arms. I'll go further. If the use of arms has any real importance or meaning in your community in terms of status and of the standards by which you live and within which you are rearing your children, then you have not only a right but, perhaps, an obligation to use them.

60   LOGAN (MACLENNAN)

If arms are a symbol of gentility in the sense that I defined the term earlier, they would be granted to you in any country where arms are still officially granted by the law of the land. But you have an even stronger claim than that; the one indisputable right to the use of arms is to be the legitimate and ac-

61   LORING

cepted descendent of forebears who did carry arms. You qualify on both scores; what you don't qualify for is the right to use the basic or unquartered arms of the Cuthberts.

(4) Mrs. Plunckett's final and very practical question might well be: Then what arms could I, or should I, use?

And this, Mrs. Plunckett, as you now know, is the most difficult question of all. Perhaps the best thing I can do at this point is to tell just how that question was answered.

62   LOWY

The obvious and simple solution would have been for Mrs. Plunckett to use her husband's arms, just as Edgar's wife was making use of her husband's. However, Mr. Plunckett was in a situation not unlike his wife's. The husband, Charles Henderson Plunckett, was not aware of paternal arms, nor was there any predisposition on anyone's part to entertain a lengthy genealogical study to establish the possibility of such arms. Mr. Plunckett, like Edgar's wife, was

63   LYNCH

64   MacFarlane (MacFarlan)   65   Malcolm (McCallum)

not of local origin, though he did come from the same state. His mother was a Henderson, a family that had and still used well-established arms of their own.

There are at this point several possibilities, all too lengthy for full discussion here. The basic problem was not merely the "bearing of arms"; any new coat would have satisfied that, and it was not the primary concern of the Pluncketts. The main point was, in view of the local situation, that if the Pluncketts were to bear arms at all, especially arms that would be passed on to and used by their children, two conditions had to be satisfied: (a) the desirable local identification should be with the Cuthberts; (b) the father's armorial connection or inheritance had to be recognized and given a position of preferment.

The solution then lay in the creation of a new coat-of-arms for this particular Plunckett family; and, inasmuch as each side of the family had armigerous forebears, there were two well-established sets of arms from which to draw in the creation of a new coat, proper care being taken not to infringe on the prerogatives of either set.

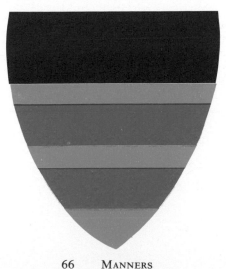

49

66   Manners

The resulting arms, by the way, were subsequently registered. What we want to know now, in order to understand this illustration fully, is just what the Cuthbert arms looked like, what the Henderson arms looked like, and finally what the new "Plunckett" arms were that "alluded" to both of them without materially infringing on either.

But before we can do this, we must take a coat-of-arms apart in order to know what its elements are and then put it back together again.

67   MANNING (2)

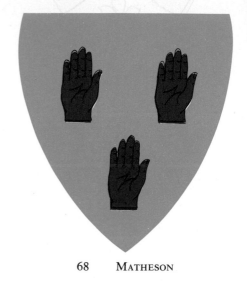

68   MATHESON

TAKING YOUR
COAT-OF-ARMS APART

The figure that you see below (fig. 69) is what is commonly known as a coat-of-arms. Some such term as "armorial achievement," "achievement," "armorial bearings," or even "hatchment" might conceivably be preferable on technical grounds, but would be an unnecessary purism.

It is desirable at the outset to establish two concepts: first, the coat-of-arms as depicted represents as complete an achievement (that is, collection of heraldic elements) as will normally be met with in American family usage; secondly, the coat-of-arms shown is said to consist of three component parts, *shield, crest,* and *motto,* although the elements as labeled on the drawing more than double this in number.

The purpose of this chapter is to explain which of these elements are necessary and inheritable in a family coat-of-arms and which are optional and/or merely decorative.

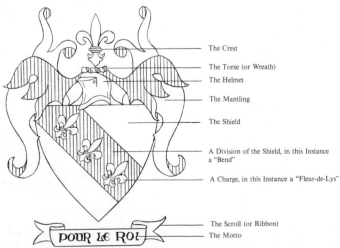

The Crest

The Torse (or Wreath)

The Helmet

The Mantling

The Shield

A Division of the Shield, in this Instance a "Bend"

A Charge, in this Instance a "Fleur-de-Lys"

The Scroll (or Ribbon)

The Motto

POUR LE ROI

The Shield

The shield, individualized by its distinctive symbolism, is the *sine qua non* without which there is no coat-of-arms; for the shield depicts the colorings and devices of the primitive surcoat (the original coat-of-arms) that set off one group of interrelated fighting men from all other groups. To put it another way, the distinctive shield itself can and often does constitute a complete coat-of-arms; it is the one basic element. Any other collection of heraldic devices put together without the shield, or its appropriate substitute, is at best so many twigs and branches dissociated from the trunk of the tree.

In the graphic representation of coat armor, the shape of the shield is reasonably optional and depends largely on the taste and judgment of the heraldic artist. Modern heraldic representation, though considerably stylized (often too much so), has reverted to the sounder practice that was current up to and through the eighteenth century; the shields are fairly simple in form and bear some vague relationship to what a medieval shield might in fact have looked like. This is a healthy aversion to the nineteenth-century convention of various gingerbread shields that looked more like ornate Italian mirrors and picture frames than like anything ever carried into battle.

Basically the modern heraldic shield takes one of two forms: it is somewhat triangular in shape (fig. 70) or somewhat squarish (fig. 71). The choice is at the option of the artist and should be appropriate to the contents of the shield in establishing a feeling of balance or symmetry. Especially where quartered arms are concerned, the symmetry and balance would be readily lost if the lower section were cramped and squeezed into the narrower pattern of the triangular shield.

70   NOBLE, JOHN T.

71   REYNOLDS II, SHERMAN BRIGGS

The Shield

Though the custom is comparatively rare in American heraldry, sometimes the basic arms are carried on a *lozenge* (a vertically lengthened diamond-shaped figure) or on an *oval* instead of on a shield. The use of the lozenge is discussed in Chapter IV, "Using Your Coat-of-Arms," and the oval is discussed in Chapter VII, "Corporate Arms."

THE DIVISIONS OF THE SHIELD

Because the "arms" are borne on the face of the shield, heralds have historically divided this face into conventional areas and points of reference in order to facilitate the verbal description of a coat-of-arms. The face of the shield is commonly referred to as the *field;* its basic divisions have been historically codified as "ordinaries" and "sub-ordinaries." It is sufficient, however, to consider both of these classifications as *divisions,* and the accompanying diagram (fig. 72) indicates the main divisions and points of reference. The word *dexter,* of course, refers to the right side of the shield, and the term *sinister* to the left. As these areas are labeled in the diagram, they seem to be reversed (as in the terms "stage right" and "stage left"), but only because the herald traditionally describes a shield from the viewpoint of the man behind it.

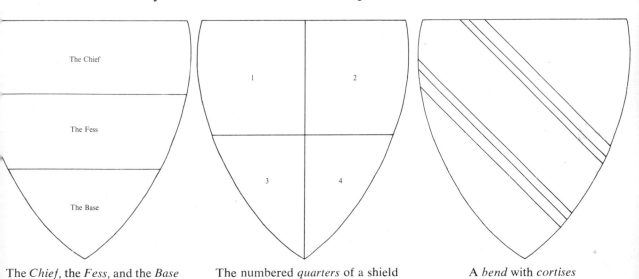

The *Chief*, the *Fess*, and the *Base*   The numbered *quarters* of a shield   A *bend* with *cortises*

72   Divisions of the Shield and the Reference Points

Such divisions as *chief, fess, base,* and *pale* are ideally considered to occupy one-third of the area of the shield; they are, however, often depicted somewhat smaller than this in order to accommodate the various configurations of a given shield and to avoid crowding.

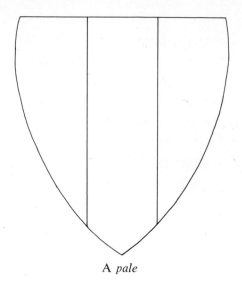

A *pale*

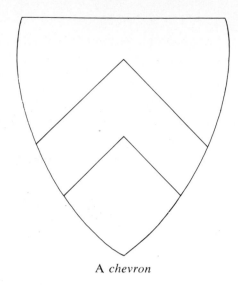

A *chevron*

During its development over the centuries, heraldry has shown more or less strongly marked preferences where certain areas of the shield are concerned. Thus, the chief, or upper area of the shield, enjoys preference over the base, or lower area of the shield; similarly, heraldry favors the dexter as opposed to the sinister side of the shield. However, these two statements are broad generalities, not universal statements of individual heraldic truth. Of the two, the first (that the chief takes precedence over the base) comes closer to being consistent than the latter. Although there is a marked preference for the dexter as opposed to the sinister side in the heraldry of all nations, the avoidance of

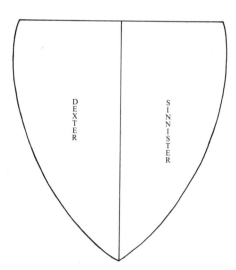

A shield *parted per pale* with *Dexter*
and *sinister* areas indicated.

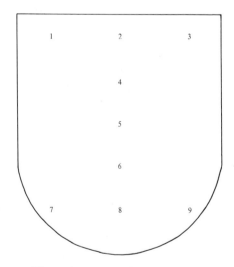

The *reference points* of a shield:
1. Dexter Chief   5. Fess (center) Point
2. Center Chief   6. Nombril (Navel) Point
3. Sinister Chief 7. Dexter Base
4. Honor Point   8. Center Base
        9. Sinister Base

54

the opposite has become almost a compulsion in the heraldry of the British Isles; usage on the Continent is not so strict and often varies, it would appear, for artistic reasons alone. An example may be seen in the arms represented by fig. 73. Each silver leaf is depicted slightly off center and leaning toward the sinister side. In all probability the original arms displayed the leaf "in pale," vertically upright in the center of the shield. Its present position is unquestionably intended to match the position of the smaller leaf in the crest; and the position of that leaf is just as unquestionably dictated by artistic exigency: it creates a better balance.

73   POLLÁTSEK-PORTOS

However, so marked is this preference that any nonsymmetrical *charge* is always presumed to face the dexter side unless otherwise specified. And a diagonal configuration, unless otherwise specified, is presumed to originate in "dexter chief," that is, the upper right-hand corner of the shield. Similarly, a vertical charge is presumed to point toward the chief, unless otherwise specified.

The lines that mark off the divisions of a shield are called *partition lines*. Though these lines are most frequently straight, as in the illustrative coat-of-arms at the beginning of this chapter, they may and often do take other forms—broken, wavy, or somewhat intricately involved. Under the alphabetical entry, PARTITION LINES, they are described and illustrated in Chapter VIII, "The Symbols of Heraldry."

Unless a bare outline of a coat-of-arms is given (a custom that was once fairly general), each of the varied elements of an armorial achievement is expected to be represented in some *tincture* (the term is used here to indicate any color or "metal") or *heraldic fur*. Now heraldry in full color, as it ought to be shown, is a vibrant art. Frequently, sometimes by choice, sometimes by necessity, color is not available in heraldic representations; for example, in single-run bookplates, in embossings, and in engravings. This leaves a choice between the bare outline, on the one hand, or some system of indicating what the colors are, on the other. The present universally accepted system for indicating the colors, metals, and furs is known as "engravers' tricks." This system has been inveighed against by more than one heraldic writer; and, though far from creating the spectacular effect of real color, it serves a purpose and is likely to remain in popular use. The following diagram (fig. 74) gives the heraldic name, the more common name, and the engravers' trick for the more usual colors, metals, and furs.

The particular intensity or shade of any given color is at the discretion of the artist. Continental heraldry, however, does specify in addition to azure (blue) the separate color cerulean (light blue).

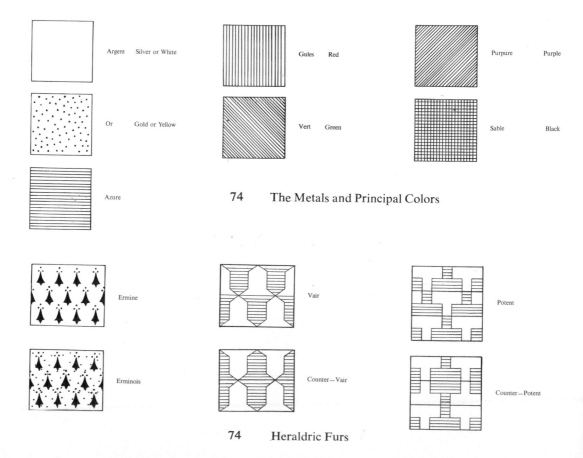

Argent	Silver or White
Gules	Red
Purpure	Purple
Or	Gold or Yellow
Vert	Green
Sable	Black
Azure	

74   The Metals and Principal Colors

Ermine	Vair
Potent	
Erminois	Counter—Vair
Counter—Potent	

74   Heraldric Furs

A *charge* is any figure or symbol placed upon the shield or upon any division of the shield or across two or more divisions of the field. A charge may on occasion be "charged," that is, placed, upon some other charge. In the illustrative arms at the beginning of this chapter (fig. 79), the charges are three fleurs-de-lys and they are charged or placed upon that particular division of the shield called a *bend*. (This is properly a *bend dexter,* that is, a diagonal configuration beginning at the upper right-hand corner of the shield. Because heraldry favors the dexter, the use of the word dexter is optional; if the bend ran in the opposite direction, the term "bend sinister" would have to be specified.) The *cross fleury* in fig. 75, however, is superimposed upon all four divisions of the shield, in this case *quarters*.

75   MANNING (1)

The range of figures and symbols used as charges is unlimited and completely uninhibited. Beginning with the Finger of God (the Father), with all sorts of representations of Our Lord, His Blessed Mother, the Saints and Martyrs, the instruments of torture associated with them, and with every known Church symbol, they continue on with the various articles of warfare (medieval or modern), with the simple artifacts of daily life, with creations of modern industry and commerce (the locomotive, for instance), with men and animals, birds, reptiles, and fishes, with—well, with everything on earth, in the heavens above, and in the waters below. Nor is heraldry content to stop there: impossible creatures, some of them often fantastic composites of known

57

creatures, are met with as casually in heraldry as Alice met them *Through the Looking Glass*. A creature half lion and half fish becomes almost commonplace next to one half man and half ship. I am waiting to see in a modern coat-of-arms, and there is no reason why I shouldn't, the symbols of atomic structure.

Many of the figures that come down to us from an earlier heraldic age have become so highly conventionalized that they bear little resemblance to their natural counterparts. This is especially true of animals. For instance, in fig. 127, page 116, the tigers used as charges are glossed as "Bengal tigers" to indicate that they look more or less like the natural animal; but the heraldic tiger, preferably spelled "tygre,"—an older spelling that helps to establish the distinction—looks like nothing at all known to the zoölogist.

Furthermore, for heraldic purposes, any charge may be of any color; with the result that the heraldist has given us what the botanist has failed to achieve —a black rose. A wolf may be green, red, or *parti-colored*. On those comparatively rare occasions when an object is displayed in its natural colors, it is specified as *proper*. Though it need not concern us here, there are, of course, good historic reasons, mostly growing out of the natural needs of heraldry itself, for these most unnatural variations.

The most comprehensive study of heraldic charges is that by the late A. C. Fox-Davies in his *Complete Guide to Heraldry*.

In describing a coat-of-arms, it is necessary to specify the posture or position of most animals and birds, because it is often only the posture of the creature involved that distinguishes one coat-of-arms from another. The special jargon of heraldry provides terms for almost every conceivable posture or activity; the most frequent are listed and explained in alphabetical order in Chapter VIII, "The Symbols of Heraldry."

BLAZONING

Heraldry makes a sharp distinction between the verbs "to blazon" and "to emblazon." To emblazon a coat-of-arms means to depict it graphically, normally in full color, although by extension any drawing or engraving that indicates (as by the engravers' tricks) the colors of the achievement is still regarded as an emblazonment.

On the other hand, to blazon a coat-of-arms is to describe it verbally. This verbal record is very much like a medical man's prescription; it enables the heraldic artist to emblazon the arms so described. Now obviously any verbal description of a coat-of-arms, if highly accurate, will serve the intended purpose. But the margin of error is very great, as you can easily discover by asking a friend to describe for you in his own words even a simple coat-of-arms, to say nothing of what will happen if he tries to describe one of the more complicated coats. And even a minor error can result in the production of an entirely different coat-of-arms from the one intended.

Just as law, medicine, linguistic, or mathematics each has its specialized language—and to some extent its specialized grammar—to avoid ambiguity and inaccuracy, heraldry, along with the other sciences—and even earlier than some—began to develop a language and grammar of its own to insure accuracy and uniformity. As used in English (and compare the language of law in this respect), the language of heraldry is heavily encrusted with terms and constructions that derive from the Norman French, or Anglo-Norman, which was the polite and educated language of the British Isles during the centuries in which the science of heraldry was codified.

As a result, blazoning has become a minor science in its own right. The twin dangers that beset any science, of course, are: first, its practitioners may become more enamored of its rules than of its function; and, secondly, (compare the medical man's prescription) it may become a conspiracy against the layman. The science of blazon has not been immune to either, but the better heraldic writers have consistently fought to keep the language of blazon as simple as accuracy will permit. When the rules of blazon become so complex that they obscure meaning, and thus create ambiguity and inaccuracy, they have defeated the purpose for which they exist.

Yet the rules of blazon can be simplified to the point that anyone interested may with a few minutes' study and occasional practice read a blazon and then picture, either in his mind or on paper, the arms which that blazon is intended to convey; and, conversely, he should, with a little more practice, be able to blazon a not too complicated coat-of-arms from its pictorial representation.

The basic philosophy of description is to begin with the more important elements and move to the less important. Remember in describing a shield that heraldry favors the chief (upper portion) and the dexter (right) side. Also, with the exception of the terms dexter and sinister, adjectives normally follow their nouns. It is a matter of small moment, but I may mention that the position of dexter and sinister varies in usage according to the noun. If the noun is an archaic term of Anglo-Norman derivation, the adjective follows (*e.g.*, a bend dexter); if the noun is of English origin, the adjective precedes (*e.g.*, a dexter hand).

Each element of a coat-of-arms is described in its own brief paragraph, preferably in a single sentence: first, the shield; secondly, the crest; and, thirdly, the motto.

It is a convention of heraldic blazon not to repeat the name of a color, metal, or fur in any given brief paragraph, substituting instead the phrase "of the first (second or third)" and meaning the same as the first (second or third) tincture mentioned in that paragraph. Normally this works out quite well; but in a complicated set of arms it may lead to ambiguity. It is better under such circumstances to forget the "conventions" and insure accuracy by repeating the name of the color, metal, or fur.

Another convention is that when two or more charges are named in immediate succession and all have the same color, the color is specified after the final object in the series and applies to all.

Finally, many charges—especially animals or parts of animals—require an adjective describing the posture, activity, or physical limitation. The order of blazoning is to name the animal first, then the adjective that describes its posture or activity, and finally its color.

All of these points are illustrated in the blazons that follow. Try to picture in your mind the coat-of-arms being described, then turn to the emblazonment (the graphic representation) as indicated by the figure and page number to check the accuracy of your interpretation. We'll begin with a full set of arms to illustrate the separate paragraphing for shield, crest, and motto. The example is fig. 69, page 51, used as the illustrative arms for this chapter.

"DE LA TOUR"

Arms: Argent, on a bend gules three fleurs-de-lys of the first (or of the field).
Crest: On a torse (or wreath) of the colors (or liveries) a fleur-de-lys argent.
Motto: *Pour le Roi*

The brief paragraph describing the *arms,* that is, the shield proper, begins wtih the single word *argent* (silver). This means, "The basic coloration of the shield is silver." It then moves on to the one basic division of the shield, here designated as a "bend." We might have said "bend dexter," though the specification is unnecessary; and the color of the bend is given as "gules" (red). On this bend appear, finally, the three charges, the fleurs-de-lys. They, too, are argent or silver, but, following the convention, the name of the metal is not repeated; they are designated instead as "of the first," meaning of the first tincture meantioned; or they may be designated as "of the field," that is, having the same tincture as the field.

A blazon of the shield shown in fig. 75, page 57, would read as follows:

> Quarterly azure and gules, a cross fleury between four trefoils argent.

Again we begin with a description of the field; it is divided into quarters, or four equal parts, and the colors are given as *azure* (blue) and *gules* (red). The first color named is blue, so it applies to the most important quarter, the dexter chief; the next color, red, pertains to the second quarter, the sinister chief. The colors are then necessarily reversed in the lower half of the shield or otherwise the field would not be divided colorwise into four quarters. Next come the charges, five in number; the first and most important is the *cross fleury*. (This simply means a cross whose arms terminate in a conventionalized florate pattern.) No tincture is immediately indicated for this charge, but it is one of a series, and the term "argent" (silver) following the four trefoils applies to all five. Finally we have mention of the four "trefoils" (shamrocks) that surround the cross. Notice that the cross is described as being "between" the four trefoils. Heraldry, like historic English, knows nothing of the modern rule that "between" must be used with two and "among" with a greater number.

The arms shown in fig. 76 are blazoned:

> Argent, (in base) a hand (or dexter hand) couped (or coupé) gules, clutching a sword azure pommeled and hilted or.

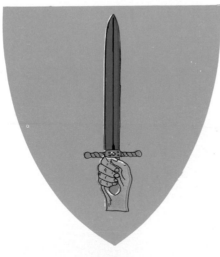

Again the field is silver. It is really not necessary to specify that the hand is "in base"; it is clutching a sword, and, unless otherwise specified, the sword is assumed to be upright, which would necessarily place the hand toward the bottom of the shield. The hand has a limitation; it is *couped* or *coupé,* which means that it is finished off at the wrist by a straight line; and, finally, the hand is given a color, "gules" (red). The sword is described as "azure" (blue), but this can apply only to the blade of the sword, for we are told that its pommel and hilt are colored "or" (gold).

The legendary arms of Sir Launcelot (fig. 77) are blazoned:

77   LAUNCELOT, SIR

Gules, a griffin segreant (rampant) or.

This time the field is red (gules); the single charge, a griffin, is named; then his position is indicated—he is "rampant," that is, standing on one rear leg and with the forelegs elevated in the position shown (and normally facing the dexter side)—and finally his color is mentioned. He is gold (or).

The Crest

There is a marked tendency for the unknowing to use the term crest in referring to any heraldic representation, more especially the complete *achievement,* or what is more usually referred to as the coat-of-arms. The student of heraldry properly regards this usage as an illiteracy and reserves the term crest for that part of the representation attached to the crown of the helmet, when the helmet is represented, or surmounting the torse when the helmet is omitted.

This popular confusion between the terms crest and coat-of-arms (or achievement), though frowned upon today, reached its height during the nineteenth century; it was met with in the work of reputable (though nonheraldically trained) writers and in the conversation of people who, born and reared in armigerous families, should have known better. No reasonable explanation other than ignorance has been offered, though three possible explanations suggest themselves. Such usage may be justified as exemplifying what the prosodist calls "synecdoche," or substitution of a part for the whole. A more reasonable explanation perhaps lies in that aspect of Victorian psychology that Fox-Davies once characterized as "ostentatious unostentation." It was during that period that the older, large "carriage panel," depicting in vivid colors the entire armorial achievement, was replaced by the smaller and more sedate gold and silver representations of the crest alone on the carriage doors of fashionable families. At the same time, the complete coat-of-arms was replaced by the crest alone for engraving on family silverware, especially (and quite appropriately) for the smaller pieces. These particular representations were, of course, properly referred to as "crests" rather than "achievements" or "coats-of-arms." By extension, the unknowing would employ the term to cover any heraldic representation.

Still another contributory factor may be the Scottish custom whereby (except for the distinguishing feathers of the chief or chieftain) all members of the clan wear in their cap the same crest-badge as the chief. Denied for the most part by modern official usage the right to display the full arms, many regarded this crest-badge as the uniting device for all members of the clan, and it became for all practical purposes the "arms" of the related unit.

But, technically speaking, the crest is that part of the achievement that surmounts the helmet and is attached to it, generally, by the wreath or torse. Moreover, in the history of heraldry it is a comparative newcomer, that is, in its present form of development. As a matter of fact, Anthony Wagner, in his *Heraldry in England,* asserts that the first general employment of the specialized crest in the British Isles was during Edward III's campaign against the Scots in 1327, a campaign that saw simultaneously the introduction of the crest and gunpowder!

Though the history of the present-type crest is somewhat confused, it probably represented a recognition symbol of a military unit leader. This type of crest was generally manufactured of leather that had been softened by boiling in oil and then molded into the desired shape. As a recognition symbol, it might or might not have anything to do with the symbolic structure of the arms as carried by the man who bore it. In fact, there was at first little historic stability to the crest form. There are families whose records show accurate continuity of basic arms over a period of several centuries, during which the crest symbol will vary two or three times. Modern heraldry, on the other hand, regards the crest as an integral and inheritable part of the heraldic achievement, and it is so recorded in grants, confirmations, and matriculations of arms.

The symbol or symbols used in the construction of the crest (like the charges on the shield) normally face the dexter. In British heraldry this is true even in cases where families (generally by special augmentation) carry two crests; each crest, surmounting its own helmet, faces the dexter. On the Continent, however, the two crests will frequently face each other.

I have a feeling that until comparatively modern times the crest was relatively rare and that its startling regularity in Anglo-American heraldry represents "addition," confirmed or unconfirmed as the case may be. A noticeable characteristic is that the symbol or symbols of the crest may frequently reproduce or allude to those in the basic arms or, just as frequently, bear no relationship to the arms at all.

In the heraldry of some nations, the crest may be as often absent as it is present. Irish, French, Spanish, Italian, and (with a peculiar modification) German heraldry show no great or universal addiction to the special crest form that we have been discussing. With the exception of Germany heraldry, the usual practice in the countries named when representing arms that have no specialized crest is (a) to omit the helmet, (b) to show a plain helmet, or (c) to surmount the helmet with plumes of variegated color. These plumes are primarily decorative and need not be assumed to represent an inheritable device.

A usual practice in the German countries, when there is no specialized crest, is to surmount the helmet with a fan-shaped figure on which the basic arms are reproduced in toto. An example of this is shown in fig. 78, page 65. Frequently this fan-shaped figure is placed between a pair of horns that have intricate and gilded points. Properly speaking, these horns are not an integral part of the crest itself but historically form a part of the helmet; they hark back to the North Germanic or Scandinavian helmet structure that characterized preheraldic days.

78   The Fan-Crest

THE TORSE

The torse, or wreath, is a conventionalized representation of what was once a lashing that secured the light, molded crest to the perforated metal studdings at the crown of the helmet. It served, too, to provide a reasonably neat finish over the line of juncture. Whatever the original material may have been in fact, the heraldic artist conceives of it as two pieces of cloth, each of its separate tincture, twisted together so as to show six segments of alternating metal and color. The dominant metal of the arms comes first and then the dominant color of the arms. Because these two tinctures were often used in great households as livery colors, it is customary to refer to this as, "a torse (or wreath) of the colors (or liveries)."

When no helmet is shown in the emblazonment of a heraldic achievement, it is customary to show the torse as a straight bar placed slightly above the shield. When, however, a helmet is shown, it is customary to show the torse in a somewhat more realistic position following a line around the crown of the helmet and with the crest properly rising from it.

All too often, unfortunately, inept artists depict the helmet and then show the torse as a straight bar floating in empty space above. There are enough necessary anomalies in good heraldry without the added burden of such ineptitudes.

In the case of certain coats-of-arms, however, this slavish addiction to the one dominant metal and the one dominant color in constructing the torse results in a set of colors or liveries not truly representative of the arms themselves. Although the dominant metal is usually quite obvious, this is not always true for color, and often a true feeling for the arms would require the use of two colors. The modern artist might, if he knows what he is about, well permit himself the latitude of some of the early heraldic artists in this respect. When using two colors, it is considered proper to place the metal between them. I cite as one example the excellent fifteenth-century Garter plate of Lord Bourchier. Here the six segments of the torse are alternately blue, gold, and black.

THE CORONETS

Some crests emerge, not from a torse, but out of one or another type of coronet. Very frequently in American usage these coronets rest on a torse; just as frequently, so far as I can judge, the torse is omitted. Personally, and on historic grounds, I prefer the latter usage; but the presence or absence of a torse in connection with a coronet is perhaps a matter of no great importance in the emblazoning of arms in the United States. What is important is the type of coronet involved. Some coronets—principally the *ducal coronet* (fig. 79) and, less frequently met with, the *naval crown* and the *mural crown*—are primarily a part of the family achievement and as such are inheritable wherever the crest itself is inheritable. Other coronets and allied insignia, however, are indicative of official rank or position, such as the *coronets of rank* and the *caps of maintenance*. The so-called *ducal coronet,* by the way, is not one of these and has nothing to do with indicating the position or rank of a duke. These official coronets are all illustrated and explained in detail, so far as those applicable to the English and Scottish peerages are concerned, in such readily available references as the *Encyclopedia Britannica,* Fox-Davies' *Complete Guide to Heraldry,* and Moncreiffe and Pottinger's *Simple Heraldry.*

79   Crest of the Chapel of the Venerable Bede

These coronets of rank, like supporters, have no place whatever in American family coat armor. Their presence (I wish I could say rare presence) on the walls, stationery, and silverware of private American citizens is at best a confession of ignorance and at worst an indication of fraud on somebody's part—usually, I believe, on the part of various unqualified (to put it charitably) "genealogists" and "heraldic artists."

THE HELMET

As in the case of the shield, modern usage prefers a helmet of simple lines and clean design and generally avoids the impossible and ornate representations of knightly headgear so characteristic of the heraldic artistry of the last century. On the other hand, it ought to be admitted in all honesty that the rococo drawings of the nineteenth century were not much of an exaggeration of the ornate "display" or "parade" helmets that were actually carried, if not worn, in the late Middle Ages.

The specific type of helmet is largely a matter of artistic choice, but it should clearly bear a reasonable relationship as to style and period to the shield with which it is shown.

The size of the helmet in a modern representation is of considerable importance, both in its relationship to the size of the crest which is attached to it and to the size of the shield with which it is emblazoned. In the case of a rather complex crest which must be rather larger than usual for its specifics to be recognizable at all, it is artistically better judgment to omit the helmet from the achievement, lest its relative size dominate the entire emblazonment. For the helmet, though highly decorative, martial in aspect, and usually depicted, is not an integral part of the achievement nor, in America, distinguishing.

It is conventional to "unify" the shield and helmet in representations by having the lower part of the helmet slightly overlap the upper edge of the shield.

Where the relation of helmet and shield is concerned, two variations from older usage should be noticed. In earlier heraldic representations, the helmet was shown upright and the shield beneath it was frequently drawn as leaning at an angle, in the general position of a bend. This was in imitation of the position these two component elements would assume when actually worn and carried by a man on horseback. Modern usage, to achieve a higher degree of symmetry, generally avoids the leaning shield.

The second variation in modern representation concerns the relative size of helmet and shield. Older emblazonments emphasize the size of the helmet at the expense of the shield, and this was in accord with the realities of the time. Modern usage, on the other hand, emphasizes the size of the shield (which bears the significant armorial design) at the expense of the helmet, which in American usage is not really necessary to the achievement at all.

Up to this point, American usage where the representation of the helmet is concerned is generally in accord with that of the British Isles or of the Continent. Beyond this point, some noticeable divergencies occur. In the official heraldry of the United Kingdom, certain types and shapes of helmets, position of the visor (whether open or closed), metallic structure of the visor, and direction of the helmet (whether it is in profile or facing the observer), may all be indicative of rank or position, starting with certain orders of knighthood. The helmet of the "esquire" or "gentleman" is designated as being in profile, (facing the dexter, of course), with visor closed, and described as being steel in color. Now generally speaking, though subject to the restrictions of good taste, all of this is meaningless in America. Much of this may be disregarded with impunity, if the artist knows what he is doing; if he doesn't, much of it may be disregarded at the expense of making a family look ridiculous. No American cares to carry a helmet in his achievement that anywhere else would proclaim his position as sovereign or as of a specific rank in an established peerage.

Although I have never seen in American usage a helmet *affronté* (facing front) with closed visor when it was surmounted by a crest, I have seen the affronté helmet used as a decorative finish to the shield when there was no crest (see fig. 80). The argument that this violates the rules of *British* usage for simple gentlemen in that it may be confused with the armorial bearings of certain knightly orders or those of the knight baronet seems inapplicable here. In the first place, this is *American* usage; secondly, the British knight carries the insignia of his order and the baronet his special badge.

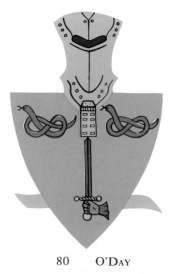

The color of the helmet (and this is not a problem limited to American heraldry) needs some comment. Theoretically, the helm of the esquire or gentleman is traditionally regarded as steel. Just how the heraldic artist is to distinguish steel from silver in a color representation has long been a problem. In engravings and line drawings, the issue is begged by simply omitting any indication of color—which omission in itself, by the way, indicates silver. In color representations, however, it has long been the custom to "suggest" a steel helmet by using some pale neutral color that does not allude to any of the heraldic colors of the arms themselves. This is still the conventional solution in American coat armor. On the Continent, however, it is not unusual to see the helmet depicted in black or in one of the basic colors of the arms themselves. In recent years this latter custom has been adopted in America as well. (See fig. 70, page 52.) This practice serves to unite the highly decorative but nonessential helmet with the equally decorative and nonessential mantling.

THE MANTLING

The mantling, though historically justified as part of the medieval warrior's accoutrements, is purely decorative; its presence or absence is immaterial in a modern achievement. It derives, of course, from the longish cloth or lambrequin that the medieval warrior used to protect his helmet and other parts of his metallic armor from the blistering sun of southern climates.

Early stall plates generally represent it with a fair degree of accuracy, and conventionally its outer surface reproduces the dominant color of the arms, its inner surface the dominant metal. To show both tinctures, it is necessary to have the mantling doubled back in places. It is presently shown as much larger than it was in the earlier representations and, depending as it does from the torse on either side of the helmet, it is used chiefly as an artistically unifying framework for the rest of the achievement. During the centuries of heraldic art, the mantling has become increasingly florate and vine shaped, the original intention of which was clearly to indicate that its wearer had been in many an active campaign and that the lambrequin had been slashed by many a hostile sword. In engravings, the mantling has frequently degenerated into little more than a complicated system of curlicues. With the increasing simplicity and dignity of modern representations, the mantling has little function or excuse unless it subordinates itself to form a unifying framework for the rest of the achievement.

The Motto and Scroll

The term *motto* as referring to the one or more words generally associated with many coats-of-arms is perhaps not the happiest term (within the modern meaning of the word motto) that might be applied. But motto it has been for centuries, and motto it is likely to remain. For many of these heraldic mottoes are not, in the modern sense, a verbal expression of one's guiding principle in life. Many are in reality ancient war cries; others are references to a real or fancied ancestral achievement; still others are (good or bad) puns on the family name. And by no means do all family arms even carry mottoes.

Unfortunately, most American families are unaware of the fact that unless the motto appears in the original grant of arms it is not a necessarily inheritable part of the achievement at all. Traditionally, the motto is a matter of individual choice for each member of the family, and in that sense it is the most personal part of any coat-of-arms. Some particularly apt or historically famous mottoes are too meaningful to discard or replace, but more American families who carry arms should be aware of the fact that the motto is optional in the first place and subject to individual choice in the second. Too many of us assume that anything that appears in the earliest representation of our family arms is necessarily sacrosanct—an assumption that extends in some instances even to the flourishes of a fanciful mantling.

To avoid having the motto exist in empty space, it is shown on a fanciful piece of scrollwork or a ribbon. Its usual place in American heraldry is just below the shield.

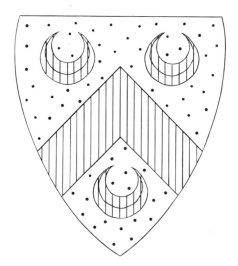

The "Cuthbert" Arms

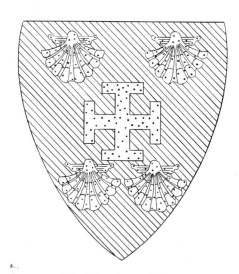

The "Henderson" Arms

81   The "Plunckett" and Allied Arms

70

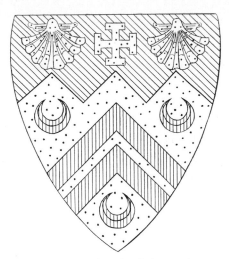

The "Plunckett" Arms

The "Plunckett Arms"

We are now ready to return to Amy Plunckett and the solution of her armorial problem. The three coats-of-arms on pages 70 and 71 show respectively (a) the Cuthbert arms, hereditary in Mrs. Plunckett's family, but to the use of which she was not entitled; (b) the Henderson arms, hereditary in the maternal line of her husband's family, and to the use of which he was not entitled; and (c) the "new" Plunckett arms for that particular family that allude to the two previous ones.

To review the system of blazoning, these several arms may be described as:

Cuthbert   Or, a chevron between three crescents gules.

Henderson   Vert, a cross *potent* between four scallop shells or.

Plunckett   Or, two *chevronelles* between three crescents gules. On a chief dancetté vert, a cross potent between two scallop shells of the first.

But we mentioned earlier that Amy Plunckett's cousin Edgar and his wife, in limiting themselves (and quite correctly, if they so chose) to the Cuthbert arms, had failed to take advantage of the several sanctions in American usage where the wife's paternal arms are concerned. Just what could be done to make use of the wife's arms in connection with the Cuthbert arms will be discussed more fully in Chapter V, "How Family Arms Grow."

USING YOUR

COAT-OF-ARMS

Where good taste is concerned, the answer to Shakespeare's misquoted question is yes, one can desire too much of a good thing. The ways, any one of which is quite legitimate in itself, in which you may use your coat-of-arms are so numerous and varied that even a reasonably curtailed list sounds ridiculous; and, indeed, anyone would soon appear quite ridiculous who tried to use his coat-of-arms in all of them. I am listing quite a few uses here for the simple reason that most American families who display coat armor do so in just one or two stereotyped ways, neglecting other more meaningful and satisfying usages.

82   MEEHAN (MEIGHAN)

One way to begin is to review some older and historic armorial customs that are now obsolete; yet you will find that nearly every one of these older customs has been adapted in some way or another so as to have a modern counterpart. For example, up through the eighteenth century it was not unusual for a person's portrait to show, usually in an upper corner of the canvas, his or her armorial bearings. In certain parts of America this custom survived even into the nineteenth century, as a visit to almost any historical museum will attest. The custom is now obsolete, of course; though I see no reason why it shouldn't suggest itself to the traditional-minded as a meaningful revival.

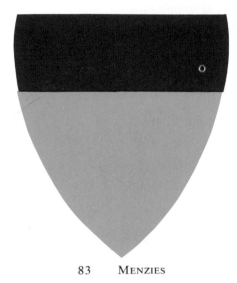

83   Menzies

But it has left a curious survival. In the last chapter we mentioned the appropriateness of our Mrs. Plunckett's hanging her framed painting of the Cuthbert arms immediately below the portrait of her grandfather. This is frequently seen, especially in the case of nonpaternal arms associated with a particular ancestor.

84   Morgan

Another and even more ancient custom was the use of "livery colors." In the Middle Ages and considerably later the owners of the great houses of Europe dressed their servants in special liveries of uniform design whose colors reflected the dominant tinctures of the family arms. These same livery colors were used as trappings for the horses as well as for the upholstery of furniture and the various interior draperies of the household. (Colorful as it may have been, it could be quite monotonous as well.) Sometimes, at even greater expense, the drapery and upholstery material was woven with repeated designs of the coat-of-arms. None of this ever took serious root in the United States, though the decorations of State Mansions and even of the White House have, from time to time, reflected the influence of these old customs.

85   MUNRO (MONROE)

And yet these customs, outlandish as they may seem today, have left their mark in modern décor. Just as the modern interior decorator, whether a professional or the interested householder, will "build" the color scheme of a room to emphasize and harmonize with the general color motif of a special painting, so often this color scheme is planned with the livery colors in mind, especially if a very fine representation of the family arms is the focal point of visual interest. In this regard, consider the possibilities of the excellent modern wallpapers in satin stripes (say of green and silver) for a family whose arms show these dominant tinctures. Other combinations come as readily to mind; these are not custom-made items for unlimited budgets, most of them are readily available. Once the basic color scheme has been determined, the basic principles of modern decoration will take care of the rest: upholstery, floor coverings, and treatment of woodwork will all follow suit.

Nor is there any reason why the arms themselves may not be used, not merely as a framed picture on the wall, but as an integral part of the decoration. For example, as the central section of a window valance the family arms may, in best of taste, dominate the tone of a given room.

Not many of us, of course, are likely to maintain racing stables; but the application of liveries to racing colors is obvious.

86   NOBLE

Another ancient custom (and one that found a certain early acceptance in America, by the way) was the exterior emblazonment of arms to identify the family dwelling. These were sometimes carved in stone and then appropriately colored; even more frequently they took the form of attached plaques of wood or metal on which the arms were painted; in some cases, the charges on the shield were "raised" figures. These had long characterized the more pretentious town houses as well as the large rural estates of Europe, and this was particu-

87   NUGENT

larly true in the urban centers of southern Europe, where even modest dwellings proclaimed the family by its arms. Most schoolboys used to know that the great poet, John Milton, was born at his father's London home, the Spread Eagle, not realizing today that the name derives from the dominant charge, an "eagle displayed," on the Milton arms.

Parenthetically, I am aware that the eagle, though not the heraldic spread eagle, was the characteristic symbol of the Roman State, a government whose pattern influenced many of our Founding Fathers; and I am aware, as well, that the true heraldic spread eagle (generally with two heads) was characteristic of the Germanic reigning houses, though I doubt that our Founding Fathers were much impressed by the constitutions of their states. But considering the particular political and philosophical sympathies of our Founding Fathers, I rather wonder whether the American single-headed spread eagle, the sole supporter and dominant symbol of our national coat-of-arms, may not owe a part of its existence to its once well-known association with John Milton.

88   O'TOOLE

But where private citizens are concerned, these exterior arms are now obsolete. However, the old custom seemed to have been revived in a rather meaningless way during the first quarter of the present century. As an architectural embellishment, many houses of that period were designed with a blank heraldic shield (or sometimes one to which meaningless lines and symbols were assigned) over the entrance or above the porch.

By and large, most Americans don't care to proclaim their identity to the public streets, despite the occasional fads (such as that most recent one in

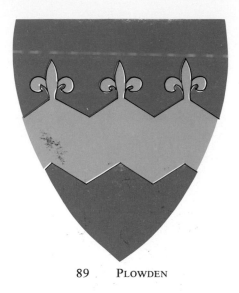

89   PLOWDEN

modern suburbia) for such items as wrought-iron lawn ornaments, cunningly
designed to trip up the neighbors' children.

Embassies and consulates, of course, still use the exterior heraldic devices.
What the average American won't do individually, his corporate dwelling often
does for him. Every city has its plethora of apartment houses that call themselves the This-or-That Arms, each of which pitifully displays some colorful
and nondescript device hoping that it may be mistaken for a coat-of-arms.
Curiously enough, this illiterate armory is not a mere new attempt at pretentious smartness; it once characterized the urban corporate dwellings of Europe.
It represents a degeneracy of an older and sounder tradition. I believe that the
oldest apartment houses in the United States are the Pontalba Apartments, two

90   POWER

block-long buildings that flank the north and south sides of Jackson Square in New Orleans. The intricate wrought-iron balustrades still bear the repeated crowned monogram of the Baroness Pontalba.

91   PRICE

At one time many of the old square-rigged ships carried painted sails that proclaimed the national arms or the arms of the company or even the individual owner under which they sailed. This custom, too, is obsolete. Your personal "yacht" may be a twelve-foot catboat of dubious design or a John Alden-built racing ketch. You may not carry painted sails; but, if you are a member of a yacht club, you probably do fly your club burgee. Many a sailing enthusiast flies his small personal pennant as well, and this latter is the one that in all probability reflects his personal coat-of-arms.

92   READE

78

The old-fashioned carriage panel, especially of the seventeenth and eighteenth centuries, made no pretense to modesty. Usually the entire lower half of the coach-door panel was brightly covered with the family arms. But this custom had already fallen into disuse by Victorian days; the great bright panel was replaced by a more sedate silver plate bearing, either engraved or cut out, a monogram, the entire arms, or the crest alone. All three of these are still to be seen occasionally on private motor cars.

93   RHETT

We mentioned earlier that the medieval warrior normally hung his martial accoutrements, including the shield with its heraldic devices, above the fireplace, or perhaps elsewhere on the walls, when they were not in actual use. And there they have remained, one way or another, until the present day. Later, of course, the actual weapons themselves were replaced by a colorful panoply that still retained the armorial devices. Often this achievement— carved in stone or wood, or painted on a wooden or metallic plaque—

94   SCOTT

remained above the fireplace, serving as a focal point of interest and as an integral part of a simple or elaborate overmantel. In other instances, especially when the arms were represented on a detachable plaque, they were moved away from the mantel, perhaps to a position above a doorway or providing the main décor of a wall or large panel.

95   SEABROOK

Millions of Americans who have visited Mount Vernon or restored Williamsburg will recall the elaborate display of the official armorial device above the main doorway of the great ballroom in the Governor's Palace at Williamsburg and the arms of the Washingtons in the "broken pediment" that climaxes the overmantel in the west parlor at Mount Vernon.

Still later this plaque was frequently replaced by a framed painting of the arms. Though traditionally and characteristically done in oils in former gen-

96   SHERMAN

erations, more modern usage favors water color—or, more properly, what modern usage prefers is a more precise and clear-cut draftsmanship rendered in India ink on vellum or a good grade of paper; the colors and metals are then applied appropriately to this drawing.

Wall Decorations

The use of family arms as a wall decoration is still their most popular and perhaps primary use in America. For the benefit of those families who are considering having a new copy made, especially younger married couples who are starting a home of their own, let me warn against hastily acquiring a cheap reproduction. Familiarize yourself well ahead of time with the "feel" of good heraldic art: study somewhat carefully those in other homes you visit;

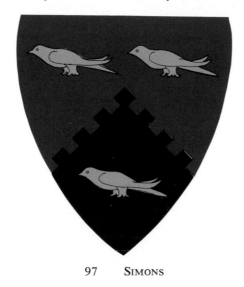

97   SIMONS

a trip to your local library should reveal at least half a dozen different styles; museums are often a storehouse of traditional models. And, finally, remember that the services of a truly competent heraldic artist (competent not only in accuracy of heraldic detail but in his artistic capabilities) rarely cost much more than the services of a mere copyist, who lacks not only mastery of his art but also is deficient in his command of the science of heraldry.

But the framed painting is not the only form that coats-of-arms take as wall decorations in modern America. I have seen quite a few examples of family arms reproduced on glazed tile—in some instances on a fairly large single tile, in others on four smaller tiles that are then cemented together. These tile representations are then set into the mantel or into the overmantel.

98   STAFFORD

A friend of mine whose father was for several years attached to the American Embassy in Madrid has as a memento of that period a wall tapestry into which the family arms (rather elaborate ones of German origin) are woven as the central motif.

More popular than the tile reproduction is the wall plaque. This is usually a polished hardwood plaque, oval or shield shaped, with the arms done in metal and enamel. In American homes, where the usual living room is characteristically less masculine in its décor than its counterpart in the British Isles or on the Continent, the plaque type of representation seems more appropriate to den, study, or library.

Most heraldic enthusiasts are not content to limit themselves to displaying the products of professional craftsmen. A supply of construction paper in varied colors, some Bristol board, scissors, paste pot, a few drawing instru-

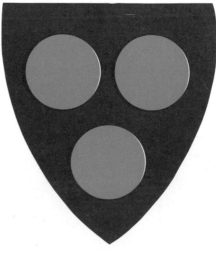

99   STANDISH

ments, and a healthy enthusiasm on the part of one or several members of a family can produce a most colorful frieze for the walls of a man's den or study. The hobbyist with a jigsaw and various thicknesses of plywood can produce highly professional results. The amateur ceramist with a knack for painting acquires an entirely new dimension of art.

100   STOKES

The arms displayed, in addition to family arms, may include national, state, city, school and college, fraternal and organizational, parochial or diocesan, as well as a variety of others. One teen-age boy has such a frieze encircling the walls of his bedroom. The arms grow (and are sometimes changed) with his interests. They encompass not only those of his real heroes, including some famous literary men, but also certain "fabulous" arms. The enthusiastic student of armory is aware that the even more enthusiastic heraldic writers of the

101   SUTHERLAND

Middle Ages provided appropriate arms for just about every prominent figure, real or imagined, who caught their fancy. The Knights of the Round Table have their armorial bearings as well as Prester John, and so do the great figures of classical literature. The apostles themselves are assigned proper bearings, and almost every important figure in the Old Testament is properly accounted for. Even Adam and Eve had individual arms! We are certainly all descended from the most ancient possible armigerous line. And, if you are interested in the armorial bearings of our common ancestors, they are described, for Adam, as a red shield with a border of fig leaves proper. Eve bore a silver shield with a solitary charge—a green apple!

102   Tiernay

Either with or without tongue in cheek, the medieval heralds properly regarded Eve as a true *heraldic heiress* and accordingly had Adam carry his wife's shield as an *escutcheon of pretence* in the center of his own. Presumably then Cain, Abel, and (more significantly) Seth were subsequently entitled to quarter the two coats! (See Chapter V, "How Family Arms Grow.") What is even more interesting, the fig leaves and the apples were what the heraldist calls *abatements*. Forever attesting to the original sinful act of our earliest parents, they were not considered to be added to the respective arms until after the expulsion from Eden.

Bookplates

The heraldic achievement has been a characteristic device for bookplates for centuries. Styles change from time to time; and Washington's bookplate

103   Tobin

with its oddly shaped rococo shield sprouting graceful vegetation in lieu of mantling and with his name engraved as a facsimile of his signature may seem somewhat old fashioned today, but it still has great dignity and achieves an amazing simplicity of design.

Modern bookplates vary somewhat as to size and shape; most, however, are rectangular, though a few are square. The color of the paper stock varies also, though those in off-white or buff are in better taste. A few have deckled edges, though modern simplicity prefers an evenly trimmed edge. Some carry a border, usually a simple one that doesn't "fight" with the arms; others dispense with a border altogether.

If you are planning a bookplate, consult a reputable social engraver (if none is available locally, it is worthwhile to seek advice by mail); for in the choice of a bookplate conservatism and good taste are paramount. Fine books, as examples of the printer's art, have "a life beyond life" even beyond Milton's meaning of the phrase. There are still quite a few of us who enjoy the thrill

104   Torrence (Torrance)

of taking down a well-rubbed leather volume from our shelves and noticing for the thousandth time a grandfather's or great-grandmother's bookplate in it. A good bookplate, like the very book it brands as yours, is at once a challenge and an inspiration to future generations.

105   TRAVIS

Because bookplates are relatively large—a size of four inches by two and a half is not unusual—the entire heraldic achievement may be conveniently represented in some detail. Your basic choice is whether to reproduce the arms in full color or in a single color. If you decide on full color, you will need several "cuts" or plates at a considerable increase in cost. A single-color bookplate permits the use of just one cut or plate; the tinctures, of course, will have to be represented by the lines and dots, the engravers' tricks, discussed in a previous chapter. This method is not only less expensive, it is probably at the moment in somewhat better taste.

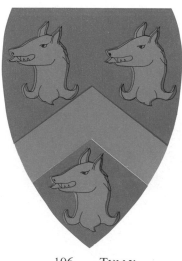

106   TULLY

For a long time it was customary to have the bookplate carry the legend *Ex Libris* preceding the owner's name. In recent years the *Ex Libris* wording has been generally dropped, the name appearing directly under the arms. Occasionally Old English or some type of Roman lettering is used for the name, but a simple script is preferable.

If the arms are presented in full color, it is preferable to have the name beneath them in black. In the case of a single-color bookplate, the color (if it is not to be black, which is generally avoided today) should be a shade of the dominant color appearing in the arms; the exact shade, of course, will be determined largely by the color harmony between it and the color of the paper stock selected.

107   URQUHART

Stationery

The family coat-of-arms has long been thoroughly at home on social stationery. Here it is characteristically centered at the top of the page and, unlike the representation on a bookplate, it is of necessity rather small. The usual dimensions, for a complete achievement, are from three-quarters of an inch to an inch in height, from one-half to three-quarters of an inch in width. These modest dimensions often demand certain compromises if the arms are to be legible at all. In the case of a very simple coat, it is quite possible to indicate the heraldic tinctures by the use of engravers' tricks without obscuring the arms. Where more complicated patterns are concerned, it is perhaps better to make no attempt at indicating tinctures, merely establishing the divisions of the shield and the shape of the charges by outline. Often, too, the legibility of the arms can be reasonably increased by omitting the highly decorative but otherwise meaningless mantling to permit an increased size of the shield. Similarly, the helmet can be omitted as well; the crest (if there is one) is then placed on its wreath immediately above the shield.

Implicit in the foregoing remarks is the inference that arms on social stationery are not usually shown in full colors. The possible exception to this is in the case of those arms where there is only a single color plus a metal, especially if the metal is silver which is characteristically shown without tricking. But even here, though the imprint may be shown in color and that the one color of the arms, it is perhaps better taste to indicate the color, if the representation is large enough to permit it, with an engravers' trick.

Most people, I assume, would prefer to have a hand-engraved die for printing the heraldic device on their social stationery rather than a photoengraving. But the truth of the matter is that the printer's art in recent years has reached a point where "raised printing" is just as satisfactory and certainly much less expensive.

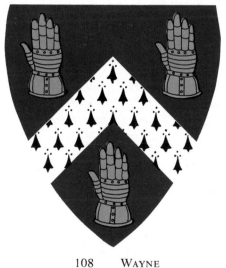

108   WAYNE

For social stationery of everyday use it is usual to have the imprint in color rather than merely embossed, though the latter usage is often seen and is equally correct. Good taste demands that whatever color is used should not be merely a matter of whim nor changed to suit the particular pastel shade of each new order of stationery. If the color tone of the stationery permits, it is best to print the coat-of-arms in the dominant color of the arms themselves.

If the color of the paper stock does not permit this harmoniously, the arms may be printed in silver or gold, or merely embossed. This is equally true

109   WILLARD

where the dominant color of the arms (purple or black, for instance) may be offensive to the family or subject to misunderstanding.

But where social stationery is concerned, the question most often asked is this: May we use the entire achievement, or *must* the ladies of the household display the family arms on a lozenge, omitting crest, helmet, and mantling?

110   WILLSON

If you have little faith in your own quite old and solid tradition, the answer is yes. If you want to follow well-established American usage, the answer is no. The entire achievement is quite correct on social stationery for the ladies

as well as for the gentlemen of the household. As far back as the 1880's (the Elegant Eighties, if you will), a quite proper Bostonian and one of the few American writers on the subject of heraldry rejects the rules of British usage that limit women to the uncrested lozenge and remarks, "We Americans set its rules at defiance, and do as we choose." His observations of American heraldic usage cover a period in American history that antedates the War between the States.

112   WOOLRIDGE

Heraldry, like language, has its own "logic," which may not in all points accord with the logic of philosophy. And, again like language, it has its own regional dialects; what is right and proper in one region might not be fully acceptable in another. And often the logic of heraldry, again like that of language, may result from historic accident. In short, the American woman uses the complete (and rather masculine) achievement just as readily as she uses her rather often masculine family name. I have never heard of a Mary Williamson, even in England, signing her name "Mary Williamsdaughter." The American woman uses her family arms as she uses her family name, as a symbol of family or clan, and places herself under its identification and protection.

One clue to this American usage may indeed indicate historic accident. Recently I examined some ante-bellum plantation stationery; several examples bore family arms. The stationery then was not at all individualized; it was the household stationery for use of all who lived on the farm. It is only the later sophistication of city life that has provided the concept of individualized stationery. And under this newer concept there is certainly no reasonable objection to a woman's carrying her arms on a lozenge if she so wishes, especially if her preference runs to rather bright pastels and fanciful papers. The point I am making is that she is under no obligation to do so.

When used with wedding invitations or announcements, the bride's family coat-of-arms is preferably embossed without color and centered at the top of

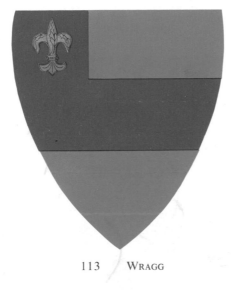

113 / WRAGG

the page. Inasmuch as, in American usage, it is the bride's family alone that issues such invitations and announcements, theirs is the only armorial device depicted. If, in the absence of parents of the bride, the contracting parties to the marriage announce their marriage themselves, they might well "conjoin" the two coats-of-arms. Or, now that they are married and the bride shares her husband's arms, they might use his alone in making such an announcement. Under no conditions, of course, would they use hers alone.

It should be noted parenthetically that many Latin families conserve the custom of issuing wedding invitations and announcements by both sets of parents and on the same folded sheet. Unlike Anglo-American usage, the invitation or announcement occurs, not on the first page of the folded paper, but on the two facing inner pages. If both families are armigerous, the respective arms of each family may appear above each announcement. In some cases the two sets of arms may appear instead conjoined on the first page of the fold. Obviously, if either family lacks arms, the presence of one set alone would be in poor taste under the circumstances.

114   WRIGHT (2)

What is true of wedding invitations is also true of other formal invitations—to christenings, dancés, formal dinners, debutante parties, etc.—that is, the armorial device may be used centered at the top of the page; and it is preferably embossed without color. It may also be so used on seasonal but non-religious greeting cards of a formal nature.

The same device reproduced in color, as on one's stationery, is appropriate on fold-over cards, the so-called informals, on place cards at rather large sit-down affairs, and on those somewhat rare but memorable occasions, the menu dinner.

Silverware

The family coat-of-arms, an heirloom in itself, becomes most meaningful when associated with heirloom silver. The inheritance and use of often completely unmatched silverware from several generations back is the pride of

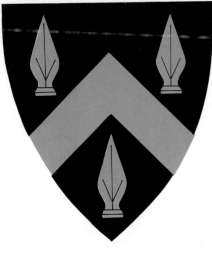

115   YEAMANS (1)

many a home. The bride who carries with her into her new home a collection of such pieces need never worry about the propriety of the several arms they may display. Such usage is always in good taste.

The problem that arises in the minds of relatives and friends who wish to give silver to the bride is whether to have it engraved with the arms of the bride's family or with those of her prospective husband's family, assuming that both families are armigerous. Usage here is very simple; you need only remember that all such presents are to the bride and become part of her "marriage portion" or dowry that she takes to her new home and her husband. Accordingly, if such presents are to be marked with a coat-of-arms at all, they are marked with her family's arms, just as they would otherwise be marked with her initials. If her family has no coat-of-arms, it is better to leave such presents unmarked or have them engraved with her initials. If, after she has set up housekeeping, she (not her relatives or friends) wishes to have her husband's arms, which she then shares, engraved on her silver, that is quite a different matter.

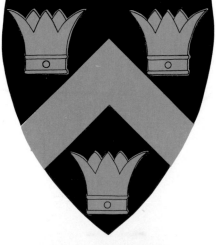

116   YEAMANS (2)

It should be noted, however, that silverware given by the groom's family properly bears their coat-of-arms.

And, incidentally, it is quite proper for the bride to bring such armorially marked presents to her new home whether her husband carries arms or not. If her husband does not, these pieces become heirloom souvenirs; the arms upon them are no longer "active" so far as her branch of the family is concerned.

Just how much of the complete achievement is to be used on any given piece of household silver is a matter of practicality and reasonable judgment. It is obvious that the larger pieces—a silver tray, water or wine pitcher, bowl, teapot, or coffee urn—will normally accommodate the entire achievement. (They will, that is, if not too ornately chased.) Each one of the pieces named, by the way, might carry the complete achievement in a different size from each of the others. The size of the piece to be marked will determine the size of the engraving. This decision is perhaps best left to the judgment of the professional engraver. In most cases such smaller pieces as a sugar bowl, the old-fashioned spoon holder, or goblets will also accommodate the complete achievement.

In marking smaller pieces where the area for engraving is so restricted that the complete arms would become illegible, it is better to use the crest alone. Many coats-of-arms have no attached crest, however. In that case the decision, if small pieces are to be marked at all, is between crowding in the arms without reference to legibility of detail or using the dominant symbol from the arms. (I know of one instance where the dominant symbol, a dolphin *embowed*, was so used on the smaller pieces of table silver. A few years later this charge blossomed forth as a full crest on the now "augmented" arms in the home of one of the sons of the family. Let me state in all fairness that I believe that many crests now in use had somewhat similar origins.)

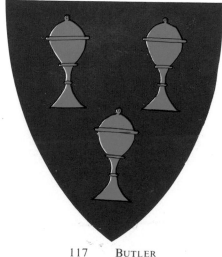

117   BUTLER

118   REYNOLDS (2)

Gifts of silverware are not always limited to wedding presents. When such gifts are made in subsequent years by family or very close friends, there is no reason why they shouldn't be marked with the family arms—or, better yet, provision made to have them so marked at the discretion of the receiver.

Such engravings on gifts of silverware are most appropriate for christening bowls and goblets, as well as for precious-metal cigarette cases and vanities.

Jewelry

The use of full arms, crest, or symbol are all appropriate for fine jewelry. A man's gold cuff links or a woman's locket come readily to mind. The family arms are most appropriate on a man's signet ring, where they may be engraved in the polished metal or on the flat surface of a semi-precious stone. Because we no longer seal letters with waxes or so affix our seal to official signatures, few men today wear the once popular seal ring, unless it is inherited from a former generation. In the case of the true seal ring, the device is cut into the metal or stone in reverse, intaglio fashion, so as to produce an embossing when applied to the hot wax. And, for the same reasons, one rarely sees any more—except in curio cabinets—the once universal silver or onyx letter hand seal.

Miscellaneous Uses

Armorial bearings are traditionally correct on fine chinaware. The cost may seem prohibitive to the young couple starting a home, but I suspect that a bachelor uncle might well find himself a frequent and welcome guest at the

95

newly established board that he has furnished with a set of hand-painted armorial service plates.

The same dies that mark your stationery and your bookplates (the latter with your name masked out) will provide gold stampings for your leather goods. The smaller one is an appropriate size for wallet, letter fold, or key case as well as for brief case, attaché case, or small hand luggage; the larger die will serve admirably for stamping the larger pieces.

As book binderies will attest, there are still a few bibliophiles in America who have special collections uniformly bound. These are most felicitously stamped in gold with the collector's arms.

The rather young men in America are not so addicted to the wearing of blazers as their counterparts in Europe, but those who do wear them often carry a heraldic patch over the left breast. In our country this felt or embroidered patch generally displays college, fraternity, or club arms; elsewhere family arms are used as well.

Finally, the old-fashioned raised embroidery of our grandmothers' day is still in the best of taste for especially fine and imported bed linens. Either the elaborate monogramming of another age or the equally elaborate design of the full heraldic achievement is as befitting to them as it is to the corner of special damask table linen.

HOW FAMILY ARMS GROW

A coat-of-arms may grow by *augmentation, marshalling,* or *enhancement.*

The Augmentation of Arms

An augmentation is an addition to an existing coat-of-arms. It is usually granted by a grateful sovereign in recognition of some outstanding achievement. This addition modifies the basic coat-of-arms to which it has been added, in effect changing the inheritable arms for the descendants of the individual to whom it has been granted. This is a highly valued honor, often more prized than elevation to one of the orders of knighthood. The honor of knighthood, in even the most respected orders, is necessarily limited to the individual so honored; but an augmentation of arms becomes part of the "boast of heraldry" for future generations to display.

In the United States, where family coats-of-arms are not regulated by law, this most unusual armorial honor is necessarily inactive; though there is no legal hindrance to any existing "sovereign" power—that of any of the fifty states or of the federal government itself—from recognizing an existing coat-of-arms and granting an augmentation.

The Marshalling of Arms

The marshalling of arms is the process by which two or more existing coats-of-arms are put together to form, on a temporary or permanent basis, a new achievement. It is the only method by which family arms may grow in the

United States. (*Enchancement,* discussed later in this chapter, does not affect the heritable arms and for all practical purposes is limited to a single individual.)

The normal methods by which family arms are marshalled are (a) by *impalement,* (b) by carrying an *escutcheon of pretence,* and (c) by *quartering.* The first two of these methods are limited in use to the arms of husband and wife—the technical term is *baron*[1] *et femme*—when both represent armigerous families. When the wife has brothers, her family arms are *impaled* with those of her husband. This consists of dividing the shield lengthwise down the middle (such a shield is said to be *parti per pale,* or *parted per pale*) with the husband's arms displayed fully on the dexter side and the wife's family arms similarly displayed on the sinister side. In modern usage this new achievement is not the heritable arms of their issue but serve for the *baron et femme* alone. It should again be noted that if the wife is not of an arms-bearing family, but the husband is, she shares his family status and enjoys full use of her husband's arms. If, however, she is armigerous and her husband is not, she no longer has any claim to active arms; though, of course, she may make free use of heirlooms that display her family arms. Nor does she possess arms that may be passed on to her children. I believe nearly everyone is aware that William Shakespeare applied for a grant of arms. He did not, however, apply for them in his own name, but rather as a posthumous grant to his father. The poet's

[1]The term *baron,* as used here, is not the title of nobility, but the old Romance word signifying man.

119   SHAKESPEARE

mother was a member of a distinguished landed family, the Ardens. Once arms had been granted in the name of his dead father, he could then display with them the old and distinguished arms of his mother's family. The irony of it is that his own reputation so obscured the social position of his mother's family that when his arms are shown today they are invariably the simple coat granted him in the name of his father (see fig. 119, page 98).

I am speaking of modern heraldic usage when I state that the impaled arms of husband and wife are not the heritable coat used by their children. In the early days of heraldry, impaled coats were inherited, as many existing impaled coats will testify.

An even older system of conjoining the arms of *baron et femme* was the more primitive method called "dimidiation." Here the shield of each family was literally divided down the middle; the dexter half of the husband's shield was then conjoined with the sinister half of that of the wife's family. The resulting coat-of-arms was always a distortion and sometimes grotesque. If we assume two coats-of-arms, with red as the basic color in each case, one of which carried three fish "in pale" and the other of which carried three wolves, also in pale, the resultant coat would be red with three outlandish figures, each half fish and half wolf. Some of the more fantastic figures in historic heraldry may owe their origin to this ancient custom. Fig. 120, page 100, probably represents one of the happier results of a dimidiated coat-of-arms that became hereditary. Dimidiation was soon abandoned, however, in favor of the more reasonable system of impalement. A curious survival of the older usage is to be found in the British custom when impaling two sets of arms, one of which has a *bordure,* of stopping the bordure abruptly at the center line. It is thus shown at the top, the outer edge, and the bottom of the shield for the arms which it is supposed to enclose, but does not run down the middle. Obviously, if both sets of arms to be impaled possess a bordure, this older system defeats itself again; here each border must of necessity run down the center line in order to show that two coats-of-arms are being conjoined. This use of the incomplete border in impaling arms has had little acceptance on the Continent; see the fifteenth-century Spanish arms represented in fig. 121, page 100.

Another method of conjoining the arms of *baron et femme* is for the husband to carry the arms of his wife's family on an *escutcheon of pretence.* This system of marshalling consists in placing the wife's family arms on a smaller shield (the *escutcheon*) and displaying it in the center of the husband's arms. It will necessarily obscure whatever would normally appear on the husband's

120 GRADY   121 ZOMORANO Y GONZALEZ

arms in the area that it covers. This is the preferred method of joining the arms of husband and wife when the wife is a *heraldic heiress*. A heraldic heiress is defined as a daughter whose father leaves no male issue. She may be the only daughter or one of several; all such daughters are heraldic coheiresses of their father.

The custom of bearing an escutcheon of pretence, as well as the very signification of the term, is much more meaningful in the heraldry of Great Britain than it is here. The English system, "one man, one coat-of-arms," obviously implies that if a man dies without male issue then his family coat-of-arms, in the particular form in which he carries them, will henceforth cease to exist. Hence, in the case of a heraldic heiress, her husband, by carrying her arms on an escutcheon of pretence, publicly states his "pretentions" to those arms; he is stating that these arms will henceforth be carried by their children and incorporated into a new coat.

In American usage where all children of an arms-bearing father customarily carry his arms, and where all his male issue perpetuate them without heraldic difference, the possibility of "lost" arms is not so imminent. A heraldic heiress (in the English sense) may well have in America any number of cousins who will carry on the arms of her family. It is only in the case of the American heraldic heiress who has no known male relatives on her father's side who can carry on the arms that this custom seems at all justified as a reasonable and just consideration to her family. Parenthetically, although her family arms may be thus preserved, her immediate family name is likely to disappear. It is sometimes continued for a generation or two as a middle name among her issue.

Once a husband has laid claim (or pretentions) to his wife's family arms—whether in England or America—he is obviously under obligation to make good that claim by marshalling the two coats-of-arms into a new coat to be carried by the children of that union. The method of so marshalling the two existing coats into a new coat-of-arms for the children is known as *quartering*. This consists in dividing a shield by a vertical line running down the center (parted per pale) and by another line, horizontal this time (parted per fess), into four sections; each section is a quarter. The upper section on the dexter side *(dexter chief)* is designated the First Quarter; the upper section on the sinister side *(sinister chief)* is the Second Quarter; the lower section on the dexter side *(dexter base)* is the Third Quarter; and the lower section on the sinister side *(sinister base)* is known as the Fourth Quarter. The two existing coats-of-arms are then marshalled so that the father's arms appear in Quarters One and Four, the arms of the mother's family in Quarters Two and Three.

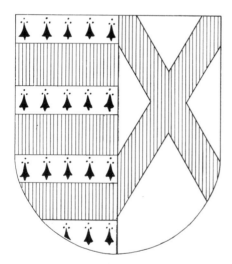

Martin and Fitzgerald *impaled*

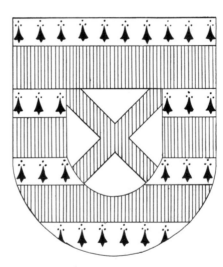

Martin bearing Fitzgerald on an *escutcheon of pretence*

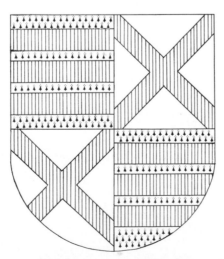

Martin *quartering* Fitzgerald

122   Marshalling Arms

Fig. 122 illustrates all three methods of marshalling arms. Assuming that a Mr. Martin, whose arms are blazoned, "Ermine, three bars gules," marries a Miss Fitzgerald, whose arms are "Argent, a saltire gules," the impaled arms (indicating no more than a union of the two families in marriage) are shown in (a). If the wife is a heraldic heiress, the conjoined arms of *baron et femme*, with the wife's arms carried on an escutcheon of pretence, are shown in (b). Their children will then carry a new coat-of-arms as shown in (c). This new coat is sometimes referred to as "Martin, quartering Fitzgerald." The arms may be described as: "Quarterly, 1 and 4, Martin; 2 and 3, Fitzgerald." Or the new coat may be blazoned fully as follows: "Quarterly, 1 and 4, ermine, three bars gules (for Martin); 2 and 3, argent, a saltire (or cross saltire) of the second (for Fitzgerald)."

If the wife's arms are already quartered, they are used in their entirety in quarters two and three. Each of these quarters, being itself quartered, is commonly known as a "grand quarter."

If the husband's arms are already quartered to accommodate the arms of a prior heraldic heiress (his mother or grandmother, for instance), then the arms of the new heiress (Fitzgerald) appear only in the second quartering for her children and the arms of her husband's mother (or grandmother) appear in the third quarter; the basic paternal arms (Martin) will still be displayed in quarters one and four.

I have noticed in American usage, however, that when quartered paternal arms have been carried by a family for a long period of time they are regarded as an indivisible coat and are quartered in toto (occupying the first and fourth quarters) with those of the new heiress.

Quarterings, by the way, are not limited to four. In a line of descent where a successive number of heraldic heiresses have married into a family, it is possible for that family to have a great number of quarterings. In actual practice, the usual custom is to drop all but the last two; the most recent heiress will be represented in the second quarter, the next in the third quarter.

One major difference between American and British usage in the marshalling of arms concerns the use of quartered arms by the children of a marriage where both parents are descended from armigerous families. The British custom, in modern times at least, is to quarter both arms for the children only when the mother is a heraldic heiress. In American usage, arms are frequently quartered for the children for the same reason that they are impaled for the parents; that is, to show family relationship, and without reference to whether or not the mother is a heraldic heiress.

This parallels the custom of bestowing the mother's maiden name as a middle name on the children. But, in this usage, neither the quartered arms nor the maternal surname seems to be particularly stable. Either or both may be summarily dropped after one or two generations. In some instances, however, this double surname (like some quartered arms) persists generation after generation so that it becomes for all practical purposes a distinguishing new surname. This is true even though the double name is not hyphenated and thus is never alphabetized under the first component. As an example, a John Overton Mills may be the son of Edward Overton Mills, who, in turn, is the son of George Overton Mills.

Similarly, the persistent use of quartered arms has the practical effect of creating a new armorial family branch, reasonably distinct from, yet clearly proclaiming its alliance to, both families. This is true even when the quartering did not originally represent a heraldic heiress. However, such examples are probably rare, as in the corresponding case of names.

This is why it was pointed out, in discussing "Amy Plunckett" and the "Cuthbert" arms, that Amy's cousin Edgar and his wife (who is herself of an arms-bearing family) did not make as much use of her arms as they might have within the framework of accepted armorial customs. Assuming that Edgar's wife had been before her marriage Jane Cruise, whose family bore arms blazoned, "Or, two bendlets sable," then Edgar and his wife might have marshalled their arms, for the *baron et femme,* by impaling them. In the event that his wife was a heraldic heiress, their conjoined arms, as husband and wife, would consist of the Cuthbert arms bearing the Cruise arms on an escutcheon of pretence.

In either case, within the framework of American usage, the children would be entitled to bear arms that quartered Cuthbert and Cruise. The purpose behind this freedom of usage (where the wife is not a heraldic heiress) is clearly to show family relationship. Let us assume that Mrs. Edgar Cuthbert, née Cruise, is not a heraldic heiress, that she has, in fact, one or more brothers and sisters. The children of any given brother will then carry the Cruise arms, which may or may not be quartered with those of the mother; the children of each of the sisters will carry the arms of the father (if he has arms), but they too may be carried, as the arms of Jane's children might be, quartered with those of Cruise. It is apparent, then, that as the next generation matures the arms of the children of Edgar and Jane Cuthbert, of the children of Jane's sisters and brothers, and even of the children of Mr. and Mrs. Plunckett will clearly indicate family relationship, even to some extent, degree of relationship.

103

All of these family arms *may* now be different (in the event that Jane has two or more brothers who have children, the arms of their children will be identical only if those children do not quarter them with maternal arms or otherwise difference them); but these various arms will still indicate relationship in a way that it would take a very clumsy name-giving system to approach, much less duplicate.

Enhancement of Arms

The enhancement of arms differs from the marshalling of arms (that is, the conjoining of two or more existing coats-of-arms to show relationship) or the augmentation of arms (that is, an official addition to an existing coat-of-arms that becomes a heritable part of those arms) in that it is concerned with the arms of a particular individual and is not inheritable.

A number of Americans have received from time to time and, in fact, now hold membership in some official, foreign order of knighthood or the equivalent thereof. It is, of course, customary to display such orders in connection with the personal arms of the individual so honored. Each of these orders has its own rules governing the special heraldic form in which its own insignia should be displayed with the personal arms of the recipient. It may, therefore, be merely noted in passing that recipients of the Roman Catholic Order of St. John of Malta place their shield (without crest, mantling, or motto) upon the white-enameled star of that order, with the badge of the order depending below. In other orders, the cross is placed on the shield that displays the personal arms of the knight, the special "collar" of the order surrounding all, and the badge depending from this collar. The one active French order, the Legion of Honor, designates even its lowest rank as *chevalier* (knight); the badge of the appropriate grade of the order is suspended from its special ribbon below the personal arms of the chevalier.

These orders are nonhereditary, and the addition of their insignia to a coat-of-arms immediately individualizes that coat-of-arms. Although it is commonly accepted that a wife shares as a social courtesy any dignity bestowed upon her husband, she does not do so heraldically and has no claim within heraldic usage to the enhanced arms of her husband. Where it is necessary in such instances to display arms for the wife in connection with those of the husband, it is traditional to employ a somewhat complicated representation known as a "double achievement." This is done by showing the husband's arms, properly enhanced according to the practice of the order into which he has been received, on the dexter side of the display with the wife's armorial bearings (necessarily on a lozenge) displayed on the sinister side. As most such enhancements will entail for the husband a knightly collar that encircles his achievement, the wife's arms balance this with a wreath of leaves for artistic purposes. To emphasize the union in marriage represented by this double achievement, both component parts are usually shown against the background of an elaborate mantle that encompasses both.

This type of armorial enhancement is, of course, extremely rare in America. What justifies greater comment and caution, however, is a type of enhancement that has made its appearance here in recent years. I refer to the practice of placing the medallion of one of the patriotic societies immediately below the arms, sometimes suspended from its ribbon. The obvious caution is to remember that such an addition automatically individualizes the arms. This is one instance where the woman who so enhances her arms is obligated to use a lozenge, omitting crest and mantling. It is one thing in American usage for all members of the family to use on their stationery the same armorial device, even in its traditional masculine form. But this is an inappropriate form of the arms from which to suspend the medallion of a woman's organization, such as that of the Daughters of the American Revolution or the United Daughters of the Confederacy. If such a medallion is used, the arms to which it is appended should be "feminized," that is, borne on a lozenge. Even then the resulting device is applicable only to those female members of the family who are themselves members of the organization. While the basis of membership in such organizations is hereditary, membership itself is not automatic but must be sought by or for the individual.

The same restriction of use applies when the man of the family carries the medallion of the Society of Cincinnati, Sons of the American Revolution, or Sons of Confederate Veterans below his achievement. It then automatically applies to him alone and ceases to be appropriate to any other member of the family except those who may share with him membership in the organization indicated.

I suppose, though I have never seen it done, that if it were desirable to display arms for husband and wife where either or both wished to carry such a medallion, it would be necessary to resort to the double achievement described above.

RECORDING YOUR ARMS

Heraldry cannot be dissociated from genealogy. Your claim to use the arms of a given family depends upon your membership in that family; and, if you are to use those arms, you must show descent through the paternal line. In countries where heraldic matters (and such matters include genealogy as well as armorial bearings) are subject to official or even semiofficial cognizance, the registration of such records is no problem.

In the United States neither the federal government nor that of the several states provides such an official service. In past generations, when families tended to congregate within reasonably restricted areas or when the various branches, even at some remove, were well aware of each other, the establishment of relationship and the common use of armorial devices presented little difficulty. With the increased (almost characteristic) mobility of modern life and the detachment of close family relationships, many families have sought to record their arms and genealogy against future use. Still others, already subject to such detachment, have sought to re-establish contact with their roots, both here and abroad.

The available resources for such armorial and genealogical services in the United States are varied and not at all centralized. It may be well to consider here, in a general way, what resources are available to American families that wish to maintain or establish heraldic records.

To begin with, quite a few of the older families support family associations or societies. These societies become repositories of family records and publish annual reports, occasional booklets or brochures devoted to one or another special branch of the family, and/or compendious genealogical studies devoted to most or all branches of the family; and to this latter type of publication may be added later supplements. Still other families publish, at one time or another, a volume of family history. Although this normally concentrates on that particular branch of the family represented by its author, there is usually enough genealogical data included to permit interested members of other branches of the family to tie in with its material.

A visit to the genealogical section of any relatively large city library will reveal a surprising collection of publications within both the categories just mentioned. University libraries, as well, often possess rather ample collections, though they may be somewhat spotty as to geographical coverage in many instances. Perhaps most fruitful of all, for that particular section of the country in which your family has long resided, are the collections in state libraries or held by state library commissions.

Every state has an historical association or society; many have an independent genealogical society as well. In some instances the two organizations are combined. The quarterly journals of such organizations occasionally publish articles devoted to family histories. The publications of the genealogical societies will, of course, be devoted primarily to records of families associated with the state or region served by the society. A visit to your local library will supply you with titles and addresses of historical and genealogical societies for the area in which you are interested. In some instances, the library may already hold files of their publications; if not, they may be available to you through the societies themselves or through interlibrary loan.

The data in all these publications mentioned so far have already been organized for you; the material is accordingly relatively easy to use. The unrelated and not yet organized material from other sources presents quite another picture. There is, of course, a veritable gold mine of material available in state, local, and special archives; in court records, in land grants, wills, church (and churchyard) records; in family Bibles, the state record of vital statistics, and in early census reports. Collecting and organizing such material is often beyond the training and dedication of the amateur. For those who are interested in approaching the subject on a do-it-yourself basis, perhaps the best reasonably current introduction to the subject is Gilbert H. Doane's excellent treatment, *Searching For Your Ancestors*.

Others prefer to employ the services of a trained genealogist. In selecting one, seek competent advice. Your local librarian, the officers of the state historical or genealogical society (especially in the area where the research is to be undertaken), a member of the state library commission or state historical commission, or an officer of a patriotic society in which membership is based on lineage (such as the Sons or Daughters of the American Revolution), will be able and generally willing to recommend someone to you. Reputable genealogists are professional men and women; they seldom advertise their servces, except in the well-established genealogical magazines.

Incidentally, if you are related to someone who is a member of one of the well-known patriotic societies, much of your work (or that of the genealogist you employ) may already have been done for you.

The same sources of recommendation are available to you where primarily armorial services are required. In addition, the officers or other members of the several heraldic societies are generally available as heraldic consultants. It seems almost unnecessary to add that you should beware of the unsolicited post card or letter or the public advertisement that offers to send you "your coat-of-arms" ("beautifully framed" is usually a further inducement) in exchange for your family name and a stipulated amount of money.

An increasing number of Americans in recent years have availed themselves of the armorial (as well as the genealogical) services of the official office of arms in the country of their origin; or, in countries where there is no official office of arms, of the semiofficial society or organization that has cognizance of heraldic matters.

With respect to family arms, the armorial services of an office of arms are concerned with *grants, matriculations* or *confirmations,* and *registrations* or *certifications.* Roughly speaking, the distinctions are these: A *grant of arms* is the allocation of a new family coat-of-arms in the name of the specific individual to whom granted and for his use and that of his descendants in perpetuity, in accordance with the heraldic rules of the office making the grant. A *matriculation* or *confirmation* of arms is the official ratification of existing arms, subject to appropriate differencing, in the name of the individual, again for his use and that of his descendants within the heraldic rules of the office of arms. A *registration of arms* or *certificate of arms* is a statement of heraldic fact. It may, at the discretion of the Office of Arms, be issued to an individual whose established ancestor had received a grant or confirmation.

The cost of these services varies with the country concerned. In Ireland, for instance, the fees are currently as follows: Certificate of Arms, £16 (or approximately $50.00); Confirmation of Arms, including Registration, £30 (or approximately $85.00); Grant of Arms, including Stamp Duty and Registration, £65 (or approximately $185.00). All of the foregoing include an emblazonment of the arms on vellum. Either a grant or confirmation may be made to the applicant and to the other descendents of a particular ancestor— a father or grandfather, for example.

In Scotland, the Matriculation of Arms costs about 18 guineas (or approximately $55.00); Letters Patent (a grant of arms) runs about £48 (or approximately $135.00). Letters Patent in England cost about £105 (or approximately $300.00[1]); the Registration in your own name of existing arms in established descent (and properly differenced) will cost somewhere between one and three guineas (a guinea is currently about $3.00 on the exchange) for adding the intervening generations down to yourself.

The following, alphabetically arranged by countries, is a list of those official offices of arms, semiofficial organizations, or approved societies in various European countries to which you may write for further information. If the country of your origin is not represented here, a letter addressed to the Embassy of that country (and to the attention of the Cultural Attaché) in Washington, D.C. should normally elicit the address of the comparable office or organization in that country.

AUSTRIA   Oesterreichsche Staatsarchiv
                     Wien 1, Minoritenplatz 1
                     Austria
I am further informed by the Austrian Embassy that the preëminently recognized authority in this field of research at present is:
                     Dr. Ernst Krahl
                     Wien III, Heumarkt 9
                     Austria

DENMARK   Dansk Genealogisk Institut (Danish Genealogical
                     Institute)
                     Peblinge Dossering 26B
                     Copenhagen N, Denmark
This institute is not an official branch of the Danish government. It controls its own fees, and they will be quoted upon request.

ENGLAND   College of Arms
                     Queen Victoria Street
                     London E.C. 4
                     England

[1]Dollar values are approximated in terms of the current (1961) rate of exchange.

FRANCE	Monsieur le Conservateur aux Archives Nationales President de la Société française d'Héraldique et de Sigillographie 60, rue des Francs-Bourgeois Paris 3e, France
GERMANY	Zentralstelle für deutsche Personen- und Familienge- schichte Abteilung internationale genealogische Forschung Berlin-Zehlendorf West Goethestrasse 39 Germany
IRELAND	Chief Herald and Genealogical Officer Office of Arms Dublin Castle Dublin, Ireland
NETHERLANDS, THE (HOLLAND)	Centraal Bureau voor Genealogie Nassaulaan 18 The Hague, The Netherlands
NORWAY	Head Archivist Riksarkivet Bankplassen 3 Oslo, Norway
SCOTLAND	Court of the Lord Lyon H.M. Register House Princes Street Edinburgh, Scotland
SWEDEN	Riksarkivet (The National Archives) Arkivgatan 3 Stockholm 2, Sweden
SWITZERLAND	Schweizerrische Gesellschaft für Familienforschung Zentralstelle Rietstrasse 25 Erlenbach, Zürich Switzerland

CORPORATE ARMS

Corporate arms are those borne by communities, associations, and organizations rather than by individuals or families. And here, to paraphrase Dickens, are at once "the best of arms, the worst of arms" in current American practice; for corporate coat armor necessarily involves, and perhaps to a greater extent than any other kind of armory, a pronounced degree of creativity and imagination. Each such bearing, whether it takes the form of a traditional coat-of-arms, a seal, an isolated device, or, as in the case of yacht clubs, a flag or pennant, is especially designed to exemplify, identify, and generally allude to the nature of the organization that bears it.

The result is as good or as bad as the capability and heraldic literacy of the individual or committee that designs it. Here, more than anywhere else, the emphasis is on "distinction" rather than mere "difference"; stereotype assumes decreasing importance, and there is little place for the work of the mere copyist.

Fortunately our National Arms and those of many of our States were designed at a time when there was still a sufficiently active heraldic tradition in America to produce coat armor that was at once authentic, pleasing, and in good taste.

If only from a purely technical viewpoint, the Arms of the Republic (fig. 123, page 112) should be studied carefully by anyone interested in the science of heraldry. Even the mildly curious should note that the thirteen silver stars, representing the original states, appear not on the shield itself, as so often misrepresented in popular display, but on the blue heraldic rose (in recent years made increasingly "cloudlike") that constitutes the crest. And, unlike

123   UNITED STATES OF AMERICA
(ARMS OF THE REPUBLIC)

most English arms, the motto is not carried at the base of the achievement but on a ribbon clutched in the beak of the supporting eagle. In fact, the presence of the motto in this upper area is reminiscent of Scottish usage, where mottoes so frequently occur unless relegated below so that they may be replaced by the *cri-de-guerre* (war cry) often met with in Scottish heraldry.

The American (or bald) Eagle "proper," (i.e., depicted in its natural colors) is a *supporter,* bearing on its breast but not in fact "holding" the shield itself.

The matter of supporters in a heraldic achievement is so poorly understood by many Americans otherwise reasonably well versed in armorial usage that a brief statement of their role seems necessary. Historically and in accurate modern usage the supporters are not, like the mantling, mere fanciful decoration to please the whim of some member of the family or to satisfy the artistic sense of the heraldic engraver or painter; they are generally a badge of position indicating continuing civil authority. As such they are appropriate in the arms of a nation, state, or city, but seen on the living-room walls of a private citizen they immediately bring the entire armorial achievement to which they have been added into disrepute. This same remark applies equally well to other regalia of rank and position, especially the various coronets distinguishing the ranks of the peerage or indicating official positions; and it applies, of course, to the special insignia of baronets and Scottish chiefs.

Generally speaking, the only individuals, either in the British Isles or elsewhere, whose arms are *supported,* are members of the peerage and of certain orders of knighthood.

Supporters are either single or double. When a single figure is used as a supporter—as in our National Arms and as often met with on the Continent

112

—it normally appears directly behind the shield. In some few instances, however, it stands to one side as a unilateral support. Dual supporters are regularly placed one on either side of the shield and holding it, or at least in a position suggesting actual support. Supporters run the gamut of human and animal life: men (variously clothed or "savage"), lions, bears, deer, and even squirrels; various outsized birds, unicorns, and composite creatures (part this, part that) seldom met with outside of medieval treatises, bestiaries, and illustrations. Even inanimate objects, though rare, may be used: stone pillars and columns.

Furthermore, when dual, these supporters need not match each other. The supporter on one side may be a crocodile in a most unnatural upright position; the supporter on the other side may be a knight in armor or a monstrous swan.

In the United States, there has been in recent years a very fine revival in the best tradition of heraldic usage by the Armed Services. The Army, Navy, and Air Force all maintain heraldic officers or special sections to design armorial insignia for their component units. And their work, as the results show, is far from a hit-and-miss attempt at originality on the one hand or mere stultified copying on the other. Somewhat modernized and increasingly stylized in concept, new charges of all descriptions are now appearing in military and naval heraldry, symbols that meet the demands of functionalism and still retain the full flavor and spirit of the older school of heraldic design.

By far the most consistent and traditional-minded heraldry in the United States is ecclesiastical, especially that of the Roman Catholic and Episcopal Churches. Though arms are occasionally displayed by individual churches of various denominations, the Roman and Anglican communions are more generally committed to their use. Each diocese has its special armorial insignia, frequently incorporating local geographic and historic as well as spiritual allusions. In addition to the diocesan arms, many individual churches in these two great historic communions bear individual arms. The practice extends to college chapels. The crest from the arms of the (Episcopal) Chapel of the Venerable Bede at the University of Miami appears as fig. 79 on page 66: "Out of a coronet or, a dexter hand proper in benediction." Simple and dignified in form, this recent crest touches several levels of meaning in its references and allusions. The golden crown at once recalls Christ the King, a traditional altar crucifix, and symbolizes the spiritual authority of Holy Church. The right hand raised in benediction is at once the blessing of the Church, the benediction of the saints, and (as a serious pun) an allusion to the fact that the patron saint of the chapel was a Benedictine.

113

Also, in ecclesiastical heraldry in America, the ancient custom of *impalement* of personal and official arms is still an active tradition. This is a system whereby the holder of an office of great dignity places his personal arms on the sinister side of the shield, impaling them with the arms of his office, which appear on the dexter side. Fig. 124 represents the impaled arms of Bishop Coleman F. Carroll, the Roman Catholic bishop of Miami.

PRIMUM·REGNUM·DEI

124   CARROLL, BISHOP COLEMAN F.

Most American clergymen who carry arms, especially those in denominations where the clergy customarily marry, make no distinction in the family coat-of-arms to indicate vocation; they follow the general American custom of displaying family arms rather than more personalized arms. Some, however, are aware of the special clerical accoutrements of coat armor. Bishops, of course, are entitled to the mitre and the pastoral staff. Clergymen of lesser rank sometimes pacify their arms also. Several married clergymen of my acquaintance carry, in effect, dual armorial bearings; this is, they display their traditional full coat-of-arms as family arms and carry the more personalized pacific arms for their individual use. The distinction between the two forms may be as simple as replacing the warlike crest and its mantling with the clerical hat, leaving the remainder of the coat-of-arms unaltered; or they may go so far in addition as to change the shape of the shield to an oval, girdled by a belt and decorative buckle. This latter feature is to indicate that they are under the authority of the Church. The clerical hat, incidentally, presents a somewhat complicated system in itself, indicating by its color and number of tassels the clergyman's rank. Traditionally, the parish priest or minister carries the black hat with two tassels, one on either side. Fig. 125 shows the arms of a Baptist minister so marshalled.

125   BRYANT, REV. JAMES C. JR.

It is a safe guess that every college or university in America, as well as most secondary or preparatory schools, bears some kind of heraldic device. A few, as we might well expect, are authentic, appropriate, and meaningful; a few are unfortunately inept and, from the point of view of the heraldist, semi-literate. What is worse, the vast majority are merely mediocre—to put it charitably, uninspiring if not uninspired.

Page 116 shows several sets of university coats-of-arms; among them the more ancient and distinguished arms of Yale University and the more recent arms of the Louisiana State University. These latter arms were designed to emphasize the military tradition of the "Ole War School," whose first president was Colonel (later General) William Tecumsah Sherman. The purple shield with the golden Bengal tigers echoes the school colors and recalls the fact that the entire student body of the original institution constituted the Louisiana Tigers, a young but distinguished regiment in the Confederate Army. They fought with honor through most of the long war and were finally defeated near Atlanta by that same General Sherman during his march to the sea. Subsequently, he fêted the former (then Confederate) officers of his old command at his headquarters before they were sent to internment in a Federal concentration camp. The small blue shield (charged with a silver *pelican in her piety*) placed in the center of the larger shield is called an *inescutcheon*. It depicts the arms of the State of Louisiana and alludes to the fact that this is a state university. The crossed cavalry sabers in the crest are a further reference

115

126   **YALE UNIVERSITY**

127   **LOUISIANA STATE UNIVERSITY**

128   **McGILL UNIVERSITY**

129   **TULANE UNIVERSITY**

to Confederate service. The American Eagle's head surmounting them attests to the continuing military tradition; the institution is still a training school for reserve officers. The motto, *Non Sibi Sed Suis* (Not for herself, but for her own), is the motto of the State of Louisiana.

The use of coat armor, good, bad, or indifferent, is widespread among business enterprises of every kind and description. It is not surprising that hotels and restaurants in this country should, as a class, be most consistent in the use of distinguishing armorial devices. The well-traveled man or woman has come to expect it. This accords with an established European usage and

116

has become by now an international tradition among hostelries and better restaurants. Related to the medieval tavern sign, this usage is an integral part of the heraldic tradition; though most writers on general heraldry seldom discuss it.

One noticeable characteristic of hotel and restaurant armory is the frequent use of the written word on the shield itself, almost invariably the name or initials of the institution being prominently featured. It is this characteristic that establishes such armorial usage as a historic transition between conventional coat armor and the modern commercial trade-mark. In other instances, the name of the institution appears on the ribbon or scroll that appears sometimes above but more frequently below the shield. Thus, the St. Ermin's Hotel, Westminster, proclaims its name on the shield itself; the Savoy Hotel, London, places its name on the scroll below.

Though the written word as part of the body of the arms (as distinguished from its appearance as an identifying label on the scroll) is characteristic of commercial armory, it is occasionally found in personal arms as well. Two distinguished examples that immediately come to mind are the name "Dumbarton" on the castle that forms the famous crest of Pollok and the word "Nile" that appears in the augmented chief of Speke of Jordans.

The traveler meets heraldic devices of one kind or another, not only in hotels and restaurants, but on almost every conceivable carrier service, where the more traditional types are to be found on some railroads and many steamship lines. The Canadian Pacific Railway encircles its heraldically authentic ensign with the traditional buckled belt, on which its name appears. The American (Steamship) Line similarly encircles its heraldic emblem, appropriately enough the American Eagle displayed and clutching the traditional olive branch and sheaf of arrows. American airlines, however, use more streamlined identifying devices that recall the types of insignia developed for military aircraft during World War I.

At least a dozen makes of automobiles carry coats-of-arms. Most of them are fanciful; some ignore the basic rules of the armorial traditions, but others are quite authentic. The Frazer car bore the Frazer arms. The arms of Buick generally allude to those of the Stewart family; and Cadillac reproduces the arms of Antoine de la Mothe, Sieur de Cadillac, French colonial governor in North America and founder of Detroit.

Stop at any tobacco counter and notice the amazing number of cigarettes that bear one or another heraldic insigne. Again, these run the gamut from the fantastic to the sound. The old-line brands of cigars, conversely, when they carry heraldic devices at all, nearly always carry traditionally sound ones.

The great fraternal orders in America have insignia of a heraldic nature; in almost every instance these designs are most accurate and in the best tradition of armory.

Every college fraternity and sorority carries, in addition to its badge, an armorial insigne. Almost without exception, these are not only authentic in design, but also far outshine the arms of most of the educational institutions where their chapters are established.

Not only do "The Old Lady of Threadneedle Street" (The Bank of England) and The Bank of Scotland carry arms, and they carry them officially, but a surprising number of American banks bear arms also. Not many of these latter, unfortunately, appear to result from very knowledgeable effort.

Every social club in America that pretends to any status whatsoever has its coat-of-arms. The older, and relatively few, gentlemen's clubs in the established urban centers are usually impeccable in their use of coat armor. Unfortunately, this is not always so true of the new family or country clubs. The first and perhaps the greatest expansion of the country clubs was during the period from the end of World War I to the beginning of the Great Depression; many more sprang up after World War II. Each one makes an attempt to display some sort of armorial achievement. A great many of these displays are shoddy and perform a genuine disservice to the institutions they represent. Inept and unknowing (*uncouth* is the technical term here) in design, they have a commercial quality that belies the social nature of the institution. To many, their shields—encrusted as they frequently are with names and initials —give the impression of advertising public restaurants or night clubs.

Finally, yacht and boating clubs must be considered; for here there is no choice, necessarily each one carries its own standard in the form of a flag or, more properly, a pennant. Again, the older clubs generally display sound heraldic bearings; most, however, are content with the mediocre makeshift of identifying initials. The most spectacular pennant of all, perhaps, is that of the Baltimore Yacht Club. It carries, as does the City of Baltimore itself, a set of arms famous in American history, those of Cecil Calvert, Lord Baltimore. It is their brilliant black and orange coloring that gives us, in addition, our name for the Baltimore oriole.

THE SYMBOLS

OF HERALDRY

Heraldry communicates by visual symbols. But throughout the centuries a set of verbal symbols has been codified for referring to these symbols. In addition, a set of directive and relational terms has grown up to indicate modifications, placement, and relative position of the primary symbols.

The alphabetically arranged terms in this section are far, very far, from being adequately comprehensive. They have been selected to let you blazon any coat-of-arms shown in this book; further, to give you a working vocabulary for interpreting most other arms; and, finally, to provide a sufficient background for a more advanced study of the science.

ABATEMENT   Any symbol placed on a coat-of-arms for the express purpose of lowering the dignity of the individual or family that bears it.

ACHIEVEMENT   The term achievement in heraldry denotes an individual's armorial bearings; a complete coat-of-arms. It always includes the shield (which may be a complete achievement in itself), the crest, and the motto (when these exist). In addition, it is customary to embellish these elements with helmet, torse, and mantling (Fig. 69, Page 51). An achievement includes supporters as well, when these are justified.

ADORSED (ADORSÉ)   A term used to describe animals placed back to back.

119

AFFRONTÉ   The term affronté is used to indicate that the entire creature or object it describes is facing front and looking out from the shield.

ANNULET   This charge is a small circular figure or ring, a sort of voided roundel *(q.v.)*. Though it occurs as a regular charge, it is best known in English heraldry as the cadence mark *(q.v.)* of the fifth son (Fig. 130).

ANTIQUE CROWN   See CORONETS

ARGENT   See TINCTURES

ARMED   When the parts of an animal that are used in fighting, such as the claws, talons, teeth, beak, horns, fangs, or tusks, are shown in a tincture that differs from that of the body, the animal is said to be armed of the separate tincture.

ARMES PARLANTES   See CANTING ARMS

ARMS   The heraldic bearings of an individual, family, or corporate entity.

ASPECTANT   A term used to describe the position of animals placed face to face, but not in the position known as COMBATANT *(q.v.)* (Fig. 131).

AT GAZE   This expression is limited in use to members of the deer family. The animal is standing on all four feet, with body in profile, but with head turned forward to face the observer. It is equivalent to the posture termed "statant guardant" as applied to other animals.

130   BECK (2)

131   RALEIGH (1)

ATTIRED   When a member of the deer family bears antlers of a different tincture to that of its head, it is described as attired of the new tincture (Fig. 132).

132   McCarthy

AUGMENTATION   An augmentation is a heritable addition to an existing coat-of-arms. Where heraldic bearings are recognized and regulated by the sovereign power, this addition is granted officially as a reward of honor and in recognition of special service.

AZURE   See TINCTURES

BAR   The bar, like the fess *(q.v.),* is a band or stripe that runs horizontally across the shield. It is smaller than the fess and normally occupies about one-fifth the area of the field. Unlike the fess, it is not limited to the center position but may transverse the shield at any point. It often occurs in pairs (Fig. 133), or in multiples (Fig. 144).

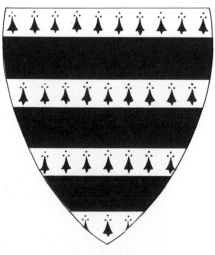

133   Washington

134   Martin

The bar has several diminutives. The CLOSET is one-half its width; and the BARRULET, smallest of the family, is half the width of the closet.

The BAR GEMEL, a double or twin bar, is represented not by stripes the size of the bar but of the size of the barrulet. The two stripes are separated by a distance equal to one of the stripes, and the two together are considered one charge. When this charge is used in multiples, the distance between each pair of stripes (each bar gemel) is increased to emphasize the unit nature of each pair. Thus, fig. 135 has six stripes; they are, however, arranged in three distinct pairs so that the arms are described as "Argent, three bars gemels gules."

135   BARRY

When a shield is divided into six or more even number of horizontal stripes of alternating tinctures, it is described as BARRY. (If the number is uneven, the shield is described as having so many bars, closets, or barrulets of the tincture that has the lesser number of stripes.) It is necessary to specify the number of stripes and the tinctures, specifying the uppermost tincture first. Fig. 136 is blazoned, "Barry of ten per pale argent and gules countercolored." When the number of horizontal stripes exceeds ten, it is customary to describe the shield as BARRULY of whatever the number may be.

136   BARRETT

BARBED   (1) When a man is shown with a beard, he is said to be barbed. If the color of the beard is important, he must be blazoned as "barbed (of such a tincture)." (2) When flowers are shown with leaves attached, or, in the case of the heraldic rose, mere tips of leaves, of a different tincture, the flower is said to be barbed of that tincture. Fig. 137 shows a heraldic rose "barbed vert."

137   LIPPE

BAR GEMEL   See BAR

BARON ET FEMME   The term *baron et femme* (man and wife) refers to the joint representation of the arms of husband and wife. Most usually this is achieved by *impalement (q.v.)* or by depicting the arms of the wife on an *escutcheon of pretence (q.v.).* In some instances it is necessary to use a "double achievement." See Chapter V, "How Family Arms Grow."

BARRULET   See BAR

BARRULY   See BAR

BARRY   See BAR

BASE   The area encompassed by the bottom third of a shield is called its base.

BEAKED   When a bird is represented with his beak of a tincture that differs from that of the head, he is described as beaked of that tincture.

123

BEND   The bend or BEND DEXTER is a diagonal stripe extending from the dexter chief to the sinister base (fig. 138). Ideally it occupies one-third of the shield, especially if it carries charges; otherwise, it is generally reduced to about one-fifth of the area. The BEND SINISTER is a similar diagonal, beginning in the sinister chief and extending to the dexter base.

138   HOWARD

There are several diminutives of the bend.

The BENDLET (fig. 139) is one-half the width of the band. SCRAPE is a special term sometimes used for a BENDLET SINISTER. The RIBAND is somewhat smaller than the bendlet, being about two-thirds its width. The COTISE (fig. 140) is still smaller, being one-half the width of the bendlet; it is generally used in pairs. Fig. 141 shows a pair of *cotises dancetty*.

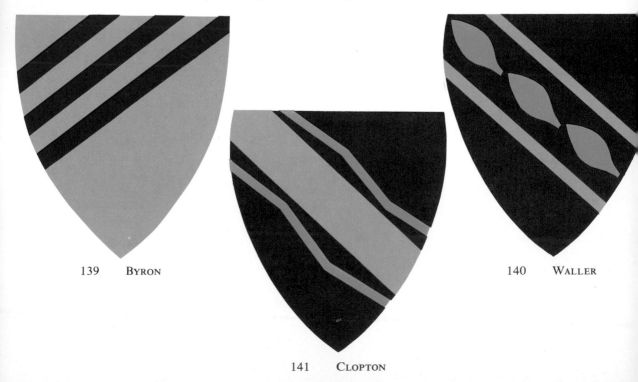

139   BYRON

140   WALLER

141   CLOPTON

When the field, or a particular area of a shield, is divided diagonally into several stripes varying in metal and color, it is said to be BENDY of those tinctures (fig. 141A).

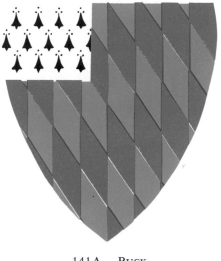

141A   BUCK

142   LEE

When small charges are placed in a slanting direction, they are said to be IN BEND (fig. 140, page 124).

When the tinctures of a shield are divided diagonally, the shield is described as PARTED PER BEND.

BENDLET   See BEND

BEND SINISTER   See BEND

BENDY   See BEND

BEZANT   See ROUNDEL

BEZANTÉ (BEZANTY)   See SEMÉ

BILLET   The billet is a rectangular figure in the form of a folded letter, as the name suggests (fig. 142). When a shield is covered with an indefinite number of small billets, the field is generally described as BILLETTY.

BILLETTY   See SEMÉ

BLAZON   To blazon a coat-of-arms is to describe it verbally with sufficient accuracy so that the original may be reproduced from the description given. A blazon is such a description. Many of the accepted terms of blazon are archaic and seem to the newcomer unnecessarily pedantic and exotic; but their validity (like that of similar terms in law) lies in the fact that over the centuries they have acquired both the centripetal force of reasonable precision and the centrifugal force of various levels of meaning and nuances in various contexts. Suddenly to substitute more modern equivalents or synonyms would introduce immediate confusion followed by a period of re-stereotyping, just to get back to where we are now. Part of learning any science (that is, an organized body of knowledge) is the process of mastering its vocabulary. It should be pointed out, however, that mastering a science is not the same (except, perhaps, at the tyro stage) as enslaving yourself to it. The question propounded by Humpty Dumpty is equally valid here.

To emblazon a coat-of-arms is to depict it graphically. This may be done in full color, in heralds' TRICKING, or in ENGRAVERS' TRICKS *(q.v.);* such a representation is an emblazonment.

The important thing to remember is that the reality of armory is always the concrete coat-of-arms.

BORDURE   The bordure (border) is a stripe that follows the outer edge of the shield. There is no standard width for this stripe, but under ordinary conditions it is generally about three-sixteenths the width of the shield. If it has a complicated internal design or carries charges, it will necessarily be somewhat wider (fig. 121, page 100). In its simplest form the inner edge of the bordure is a straight-flowing line that parallels at all points the outer edge of the shield; and, of course, the outer edge of the bordure is always coincident with the outer edge of the shield itself. The inner edge, however, may use any one of the several PARTITION LINES *(q.v.).* Fig. 143 shows a "bordure engrailed."

The bordure is found in very early armory; it was probably the first means of indicating DIFFERENCE *(q.v.)* and is still the basis for the complicated Scottish system of differencing.[1]

Closely related to the bordure, in origin a diminutive and variant form of it, is the ORLE. This is a smaller stripe that parallels the outer edge of the shield but is slightly recessed from it, showing a small part of the field between itself and the edge. When a number of small charges are arranged in a similar pattern, they are said to be IN ORLE.

The TRESSURE is a variant of the orle. It is almost always borne double, each stripe necessarily quite thin and showing a small space between them. The most famous tressure in heraldry, of course, is that borne on the royal arms of Scotland. It is a "tressure fleury-counter-fleury," which means that it is transversed by a series of FLEURS-DE-LYS *(q.v.)* that alternate in pointing inward and outward. Granted as an augmentation, it is the most highly prized addition of honor in Scottish armory.

BROAD ARROW   The broad arrow of heraldry is represented by a large and heavy metal arrowhead, regularly depicted without an accompanying shaft (fig. 144). Thrown by a machine, it was the basic artillery missile of the Middle Ages.

CABOSHED   This term describes a full-faced view of an animal's head with none of the neck showing. It is usually associated with members of the deer family (fig. 145).

[1]The scheme of cadency as now used by the Lyon King in Scotland is illustrated in Fox-Davies' *Complete Guide to Heraldry,* page 503.

144   WALSH

145   MACKENZIE

CADENCE MARKS   These are minor additions to a coat-of-arms to distinguish the various sons of a given individual. The system of indicating cadency varies in different countries. The English system is given here because it has exerted some impact on American heraldry in the past half century. Nine symbols are assigned as follows: First son, the LABEL; second, the CRESCENT; third, the MULLET (SCOTTISH STAR); fourth, the MARTLET; fifth, the ANNULET; sixth, the FLEUR-DE-LYS; seventh, the (heraldic) ROSE; eighth, the CROSS MOLINE; and ninth, the DOUBLE-QUARTREFOIL. Each of these symbols is explained more fully under its own entry. When used as a mark of cadency, each such symbol is characteristically placed in the upper-central portion of the shield and covers, to the extent of its size, a portion of whatever else occupies that space.

CANTING ARMS   Canting arms, or *armes parlantes* (i.e., talking arms), are those whose symbols suggest or pun upon the family name; for example, one or more lions on the arms of a family named Lyon or pieces of rope tied in knots for a family named Knott. In these instances the pun is obvious; in other cases the allusions are obscured by semantic change or because they were originally made in another language. As a result, many arms that were canting in origin are unrecognized as such today. Few modern Americans will recognize the fish on the arms of Lucy (fig. 146) as "lucies," *i.e.,* pikes; or those on the arms of Roche (fig. 147) as the carp ("roach"). The "fusils" (see LOZENGE) in the arms of Montagu pun on the family name as *mont aigu, i.e.,* "sharp-pointed mountain." The bay leaves that characterize the various versions of the Noble arms (fig. 70, page 52) and (fig. 86, page 75) are meaningless today; but the bay tree is also the laurel tree which in Anglo-Norman was called the *lorier noble* (noble laurel) or simply *l'arbre noble* (the noble tree). One Snooks family carries an oak tree bearing seven acorns (fig. 148, page 129); another carries seven acorns without the tree (fig. 149, page 129). This

146   LUCY

147   ROACH (ROCHE)

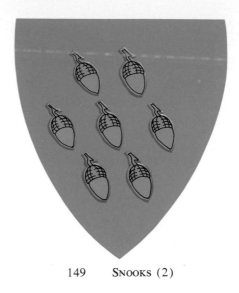

148   SNOOKS (1) (SENNOCKS)   149   SNOOKS (2)

is meaningless until we know that the name Snooks is an abbreviated form of seven oaks. These cants seldom show regard for etymological exactitude. Arms of families named Pearson or Pierson often show the *sun piercing* the darkness.

The degree of cant will vary with the ingenuity of the herald. The spear on the arms of Shakespeare (fig. 119, page 98) is a partial cant; no effort is made to indicate the act of shaking. But the *broken* spear on the arms of Breakspear goes one step further. The arms of Lockhart are in fact a rebus (fig. 150). Perhaps the most complete cant is that used as the arms of Stanford (fig. 151). Sanford (from the Old English for stone ford) indicates a place where a river may be crossed by means of stepping stones. The field is a green meadow; the wavy blue bend is a river, and the three *plates* (roundels argent), are obviously the stones used for fording it.

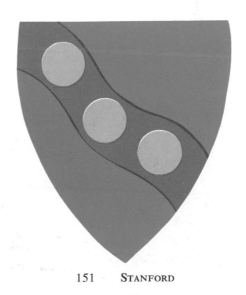

150   LOCKHART   151   STANFORD

129

CHARGE   Any figure or symbol used on the shield as a distinguishing part of a coat-of-arms is a charge. It is considered to be placed on the shield, and, in this respect, it differs technically from a DIVISION of the shield *(q.v.)*.

CHECKY   Any area that is composed of alternate squares of metal and color or fur in more than one row is described as checky (fig. 152). It is necessary, of course, to stipulate the tinctures. If it makes a difference as to how many rows should be represented, the number of rows should be stipulated. If it makes a difference as to the number of squares in each row, that too should be stipulated. If the first square on the dexter side of the top row is a color, then that should be named before the alternating metal, thus "A fess checky, gules and or."

152   BOYD

A *single* row of alternate squares of metal and color or fur is described as COMPONY rather than "checky."

CHEVRON   This basic division of the shield, as its name implies, is shaped like a rafter (fig. 153, page 131). Whenever possible, its ideal proportion is one-third of the shield. As a practical matter, its height on the shield and its width are both subject in representation to artistic balance. When the field is divided into an equal number of chevrons, the shield is then described as CHEVRONNY. Or the shield may be divided into two tinctures, the line of division following the shape of a CHEVRON, in which case the shield is described as PARTED PER CHEVRON (fig. 70, page 52). Fig 154, page 131 shows a shield PARTED PER

CHEVRON EMBATTLED, and fig. 155 shows one PARTED PER CHEVRON IN-VECTED. When small charges are arranged to follow the lines of an inverted V, they are said to be IN CHEVRON (fig. 156).

153   BLAKE (1)

154   HUTSON

155   MACDONOGH (MACDONOUGH)

156   STACKHOUSE

The most usual diminutive of the CHEVRON is the CHEVRONEL (fig. 81, page 71), one half the size of the larger figure. It most frequently appears in pairs or threes. A less usual diminutive is the COUPLE-CLOSE, one half the size of the CHEVRONEL; it regularly occurs in multiples and the figures are often interlaced.

CHEVRONEL   See CHEVRON

CHEVRONNY   See CHEVRON

CHIEF   The chief is one of the primary divisions of a shield and comprises its upper third (fig. 157). The chief is an area of preferment and honor, often used for displaying AUGMENTATIONS *(q.v.)*.

157   BRUCE

CINQUEFOIL   See CLOVERS

CLOSE   A term used to describe the position of a bird with wings at rest, that is, close to the body (fig. 130, page 120).

CLOSET   See BAR

CLOVERS   Of the various foliate herbs used in armorial representations, the most frequent, because of its obvious religious connotation, is the TREFOIL, the shamrock or three-leaf clover (fig. 75, page 57). Such variant forms as the QUATREFOIL, the four-leaf clover, and the CINQUEFOIL, with five leaves (fig. 158), are less frequent. A rare and unusual variant, the DOUBLE-QUATREFOIL, showing eight leaves, as in the accompanying illustration (fig. 159) is, in English heraldry, the cadence mark assigned to the ninth son.

158   HERIOT   159   The Double Quatrefoil

COMBATANT   A term used to indicate that two beasts are in the act of fighting. They are conventionally represented facing one another, each in the posture known as RAMPANT *(q.v.).* The outstretched paw of each is close to, but not touching, that of the other (fig. 160).

160   HYNES

COMPONY   See CHECKY

CORONETS   The coronet or small crown that is best known in American usage is the crest coronet. Many family crests rise out of a coronet instead of resting on a TORSE *(q.v.).* These coronets are of various types, and the particular kind is always specified in the blazon of an achievement that includes one. By far the most frequently used is the ducal coronet (which does not indicate the rank of duke); it is sometimes called merely a diadem. Fig. 79, page 66 illustrates a *ducal coronet* out of which rises a hand in benediction. Less frequently met are the *mural crown,* generally associated with communities (an embattled crown resembling the top of a tower and divided into rectangular designs to suggest masonry); the *naval crown,* a simple rim on which are shown alternate stern and bow-on views of an old-fashioned sailing ship; and the *eastern crown,* also called the *antique crown,* a plain circlet surmounted by five sharp triangles.

The *Coronets of Rank,* as used in the British Isles and on the Continent, are special forms that indicate the bearer has a special position and title in the peerage. They are readily distinguished by the *cap,* usually red, that lines them. Only the specific individual holding the particular title indicated by such a coronet of rank has any claim to display it. Their use in America is ridiculous and unwarranted.

Coronets of various kinds, however, are often used as charges on the shield itself. The antique (or eastern) crown is shown in fig. 161; and even a royal crown appears, for good historic reasons, in the arms shown in fig. 162.

161   McArthur

162   Douglas

COTISE   See BEND

COUCHANT   This term describes a four-footed beast in the act of lying down. The animal is represented in profile, normally facing the dexter, body flat against the ground, but with head erect and also in profile. If the head is in any other position, that position must be specified. (See GUARDANT.) When a member of the deer family is represented in this position, he is described as LODGED rather than couchant.

COUNTERCHANGED   See COUNTERCOLORED

COUNTERCHARGED   See COUNTERCOLORED

COUNTERCOLORED   Often when a shield, or area of a shield, is PARTED (*i.e.,* divided into a recognized heraldic pattern) into an area of metal and another area of color, the charges are arranged so that those appearing on the metallic part are in the basic color of the arms and those appearing on the color are shown in the basic metal. The charges are then said to be COUNTERCOLORED, COUNTERCHANGED, or COUNTERCHARGED (fig. 163, page 135). A charge that lies across the partition line between such areas is said to be COUNTERCOLORED if the part of the charge that shows against the metal is in the basic color and the part that shows against the color is depicted in the basic metal (fig. 164).

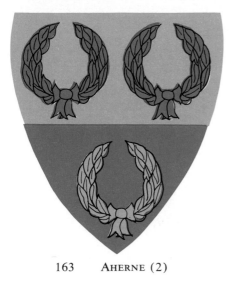

163   AHERNE (2)

164   CROSLAND (CROSSLAND)

COUNTER-POTENT   See HERALDIC FURS

COUNTER-SALIENT   See SALIENT

COUNTER-VAIR   See HERALDIC FURS

COUPED (COUPÉ)   When only part of a creature (animal or human) is shown, that part is blazoned as couped or coupé if the representation of it is finished off with a straight line, as though the member had been neatly severed from the body. Fig. 76, page 61 depicts a hand couped at the wrist.

COUPLE-CLOSE   See CHEVRON

COURANT   A term used to describe an animal in the act of running. Customarily, the body is horizontal, or nearly so, and the forelegs are extended. One or both of the rear legs may be touching the ground, or they, too, may be extended (fig. 165).

165   BRISCOE

COWARD (COUÉ)   This is a term used to indicate that the animal it describes is represented with his tail between his legs.

CRESCENT   The crescent in heraldry is represented by the embowed moon with her points turned upward. Though it frequently occurs as a charge (fig. 166), it is, in English heraldry, the *cadence mark (q.v.)* of the second son. When it is depicted with the points facing the dexter side of the shield, it is known as an INCRESCENT; with the points facing toward the sinister, it is called a DECRESCENT.

166   SETON (SEATON)

CREST   The term crest applies properly only to those heredity symbols that surmount the helmet in a complete ACHIEVEMENT *(q.v.)* (fig. 69, page 51). It usually rests on a *wreath* or TORSE *(q.v.)* or rises out of a CORONET *(q.v.)*.

CREST CORONET   See CORONETS

CRESTED   When a gamecock or similar fowl is to be depicted with the comb of a tincture that differs from that of the head, it is blazoned as crested of that tincture.

CRI-DE-GUERRE   See MOTTO

CROSS   The cross in its many variations is the most frequent symbol in armory. Where the shield is concerned, the cross is used both as a DIVISION *(q.v.)* and as a CHARGE *(q.v.)*. It is used also as a crest symbol.

136

As a division of the shield, the cross always extends to the edges of the shield. Its two basic forms are the cross, simply so blazoned, and the SALTIRE or CROSS SALTIRE, also referred to as ST. ANDREW'S CROSS or ST. PATRICK'S CROSS. The simple cross consists of two bands crossing each other at right angles in the center of the shield; one is vertical and the other horizontal (fig. 167). The SALTIRE is formed by diagonal bands crossing each other at the center of the shield (fig. 168).

167   BURKE   168   FITZPATRICK

When the arms of a cross do not terminate with the edges of the shield, the cross is considered to be a charge. If each arm ends with a straight line, the cross is said to be COUPED or COUPÉ (q.v.). This is the familiar emblem of the Red Cross, whose shield simply reverses the colors of the national arms of Switzerland. It is impossible to consider in detail the great variety of crosses that have been used in armory. Any good dictionary will list and picture up to a score; some of the older books on heraldry give as many as two hundred—mostly minor variants of a few basic patterns. Listed here are the CROSS POTENT, the CROSS-CROSSLET, the CROSS FLEURY, the CROSS MOLINE, and the CROSS PATTÉ.

CROSS-CROSSLET   This unusual cross, associated originally with the papal states, is really five crosses in one. To the plain, square right-angled cross with plain ends is added a small transverse bar on each arm, so that each arm becomes in turn a smaller cross in its own right (fig. 169, page 138). When a shield is strewn with an indefinite number of small cross-crosslets, the field is said to be CRUSILY (fig. 170, page 138).

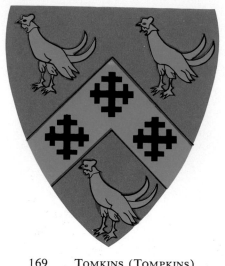

169   Tomkins (Tompkins)   170   Holbrook

CROSS FLEURY   See FLEURY

CROSS MOLINE   This is a right-angled cross with arms of equal length (fig. 171), whose characteristic is the fishtail termination of each arm. The name itself is a rather obscure allusion in modern times; it implies a resemblance to the rind of a millstone. In English heraldry this cross is the cadence mark of the eighth son.

171   Beck (1)   172   Hannon

CROSS PATTÉ   The cross patte is a square, right angled cross whose arms are smaller at the center than at their terminations (fig. 172).

CROSS POTENT   The medieval crutch, called a *potente,* was fitted with a small crossbar at the top that gave the upper end a T- or tau-shaped appearance. The heraldic cross whose arms are so represented at their ends is called a cross potent (fig. 130, page 120).

CRUSILY   See SEMÉ

DECRESCENT   See CRESCENT

DEMI-   When prefixed to the name of a charge, the term demi- indicates that only the front or upper half is to be displayed. A "demi-lion" is shown as the crest of fig. 73, page 55.

DEXTER   The right side of the shield with reference to the man who is carrying the shield before him, therefore the left side of the shield from the view of the observer. This is the honor side of the shield.

DIADEM   See CORONETS

DIFFERENCE   Technically speaking, a difference in heraldry is anything that sets apart one coat of arms from another. It may involve nothing more than CADENCE MARKS (*q.v.*) that differentiate between separate sons of the same individual. It may involve permanent additions, such as the bordures of the Scottish system that separate different branches of a family. Or it may involve structural differences in the bearings themselves to indicate cognate branches of a family.

DISPLAYED   A term used to describe the position of a bird, almost invariably an eagle, with wings elevated and expanded, with legs spread, and with the head turned in profile (to the dexter). An eagle displayed is the sole supporter of the Arms of the Republic (fig. 123, page 112). The eagle displayed is frequently met with as a charge (fig. 173).

DIVISIONS OF THE SHIELD   Most writers on armory place great emphasis on the classifications that cover the divisions of a shield, designating some configurations "honorable ordinaries" and others "secondary ordinaries." The implication is that these, being early divisions in the history of armory, therefore enjoy a position of special importance. The implication is relatively true, but only with reference to the historic study of general armory. The *inference*, however, is that the mere presence of one or more of these divisions in a particular coat-of-arms confers prestige and indicates old and distinguished bearings. But the inference is not true. The plain fact is that a grant of arms made today or tomorrow might well contain one or several of these early divisions. And the mere fact that a coat-of-arms is old does not necessarily carry an attribute of distinction. The basic truth, as was well understood in earlier days, is that the bearer distinguishes the arms, not the reverse. The bearing of arms without a concommittant obligation makes arms meaningless.

Another difficulty with these traditional classifications of the divisions of a shield is that some of the figures might be considered more properly as *charges* than as *divisions* of the shield. Their eventual inclusion in such a list grows out of complicated historic reasons that cannot be fully discussed here.

But, for whatever it is worth, here are the traditional classifications. The ORDINARIES, also called the HONORABLE ORDINARIES, are the CHIEF, PALE, FESS, BEND, CHEVRON, CROSS, and SALTIRE. The SUBORDINARIES, also called SUBORDINATE ORDINARIES and SECONDARIES, are the QUARTER, CANTON, INESCUTCHEON, BORDURE, ORLE, TRESSURE, FLANCHE, LOZENGE, MASCLE, RUSTRE, FUSIL, GYRON, FRET, BILLET, and ROUNDEL.

Each item on this list is discussed more fully in its proper listing in this section.

DORMANT   This term describes a four-footed beast in the act of sleeping. The animal is represented in profile, normally facing the dexter, body flat against the ground, and the head depressed so as to rest upon the ground or upon the extended forelegs. The position of the head differentiates dormant from COUCHANT (*q.v.*).

DOUBLE-QUATREFOIL   See CLOVERS

DUCAL CORONET   See CORONETS

EASTERN CROWN   See CORONETS

EMBLAZON(MENT)   See BLAZON

EMBOWED   The term embowed describes anything arched into a roughly semicircular shape with the ends pointing downward. It is a favorite way of displaying fish or marine animals, especially the dolphin (fig. 78, page 65).

ENDORSE   See PALE

ENGRAVERS' TRICKS   It is generally preferable to display heraldic bearings in color. When this is impracticable, it is traditionally correct to represent the bearings in outline with no effort to indicate tinctures. For a long time this was the preferred method when no color was used. Modern preference, however, clearly is to indicate the colors in a monochrome rendering by means of the lines, dots, and figures generally known as engravers' tricks. A number of such systems existed in earlier days; the one in use now has been the universally accepted standard since the late seventeenth century. It may well be that the various conflicting systems in use prior to that date were responsible for the then preferable use of bare outline; under conflicting systems the indications of color would readily become misleading.

Fig. 74, page 56 illustrates the engravers' tricks for the principal metals, colors, and furs. Two additional tinctures (*murrey* and *tenné*) are described under the entry TINCTURES (*q.v.*). Two additional furs (*ermines* and *pean*) are discussed under HERALDIC FURS (*q.v.*).

Many writers speak of TRICKING or HERALDS' TRICKS as a means of indicating the tinctures of arms. This system, however, is used for record purposes only, never for display of arms. It consists merely in an outline drawing of the arms with colors indicated by abbreviations of their names being inserted in the appropriate areas or, when these areas are too small, by an arrow leading from the name of the color to the applicable point on the arms. The usual abbreviations are: *Ar* for argent, *Or,* which needs no abbreviation, *Gu* for gules, *Az* for azure (but more frequently *B* for blue, to avoid confusion with *Ar*), *Sa* for sable, *Purp* for purpure, and *Ppr* for proper. The furs are generally spelled out in full.

ERADICATED   A tree or shrub is described as eradicated if it is depicted with the roots showing, as though it had been pulled up from the ground— roots and all.

141

ERASED   When only part of a creature (animal or human) is shown, that part is blazoned as erased if the representation of it is finished off with a stylized form of three jagged points, as though the member had been forceably torn from the body (fig. 174).

174   PRATT

ERECT   When a charge that might otherwise be presumed to occupy a horizontal position (or in case of doubt) is to be shown in a vertical position, it is described as erect. A fish in the erect position is frequently described as HAURIANT *(q.v.)*. When predatory animals are pictured as erect (fig. 175), both rear feet are shown as though touching the ground, and usually one foreleg is elevated and one depressed; all this is to avoid confusion with the positions known as RAMPANT *(q.v.)* and SALIENT *(q.v.)*.

175   CARROLL

ERMINE   See HERALDIC FURS

ERMINES   See HERALDIC FURS

ERMINOIS   See HERALDIC FURS

ESCALLOP   See SHELLS

ESCUTCHEON   An escutcheon is simply a shield or shieldlike figure. Older writers on armory generally prefer it to the English term shield. It is the normal configuration on which a coat-of-arms is represented. It also occurs, however, as a charge. When it does, the term INESCUTCHEON is perhaps preferable in establishing a distinction (fig. 176). The use of the term escutcheon in the phrase "escutcheon of pretence" *(q.v.)* does not vitiate this distinction; for this is not a "charge," but rather a complete coat-of-arms conjoined with another.

176   HAY

ESCUTCHEON OF PRETENCE   When the wife is a HERALDIC HEIRESS *(q.v.)*, her arms are joined with those of her husband, not by IMPALEMENT *(q.v.)*, but by being borne of an escutcheon of pretence. Her family arms are shown on a shield (escutcheon) which is then displayed in the center of her husband's shield (fig. 122, page 101).

ESTOILE   See STAR

FESS   This primary division of the shield consists of a wide band or stripe that crosses the center of the shield horizontally and ideally occupies about

143

one-third of the area (fig. 177). If several charges are represented in chief and/or base, the fees is customarily drawn somewhat smaller to accommodate them.

When two or more charges are placed next to each other across the center of the shield, they are said to be IN FESS (fig. 178).

When a shield is divided horizontally at the center point into areas of two tinctures, it is said to be PARTED PER FESS (fig. 179).

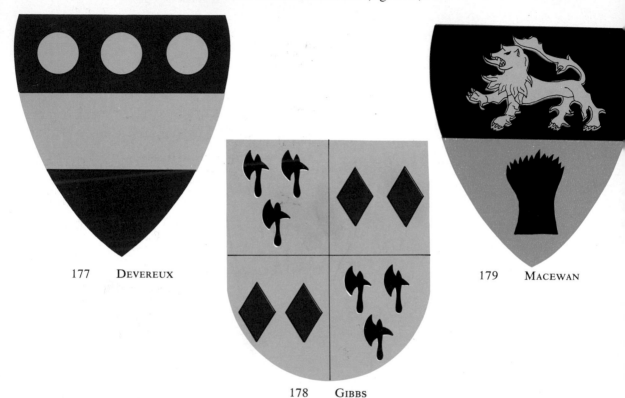

177   DEVEREUX

178   GIBBS

179   MACEWAN

FETTERLOCK   The medieval fetterlock (the term PADLOCK refers to the same figure) is represented in armory by a straight bar to whose ends is attached a U-shaped rod in some instances or a U-shaped chain in others (fig. 150, page 129).

FIELD   A term used to refer to the complete face of the shield or to its tincture.

FIMBRIATED   This term describes the fact that a division of a shield, such as a chevron, bend, or cross, is outlined with a very narrow border of a different tincture.

144

FITCHY   When a cross has its lower arm pointed so that it might be im-
planted or fixed (French *fiché*) in the ground, it is described as fitchy. When
so represented, the low arm of the cross is generally shown as longer than the
others. The cross-crosslet fitchy is shown in fig. 180; the cross patté fitchy in
fig. 181.

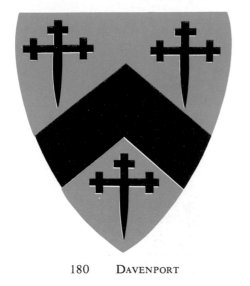

180   DAVENPORT   181   RUST

FLANCHE   The flanche is a division of the shield enclosed by an arc that
uses the side of the shield as its base. Its innermost extent does not reach the
center of the shield. Flanches are always borne in pairs, as in the accompanying illustration (fig. 182).

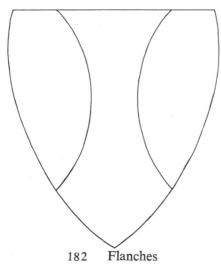

182   Flanches

FLEUR-DE-LYS   The heraldic fleur-de-lys is an ornate and highly conventionalized form of the lily flower (fig. 69, page 51). In English heraldry it

145

is the cadence mark of the sixth son. Though the fleur-de-lys as a charge and crest symbol is met with in the heraldry of all European nations, it derives from French armory, where its primary association is with the royal arms. Curiously enough, in origin it may not have represented the lily at all; more likely it developed gradually out of the "golden bees" associated with Clovis (c.465-A.D.511) in prearmorial days.

The natural LILY, so represented, is also met with, especially in ecclesiastical heraldry, where it is the symbol of the Blessed Virgin.

FLEURY (FLORY)   The term fleury describes any termination figured in a conventional florate design, usually represented by three petal-like figures. The CROSS FLEURY *(q.v.)* is a square right-angled cross whose arms are so terminated (fig. 183).

183   LATIMER

FOUNTAIN   See ROUNDEL

FRET   The rather intricate figure known as the fret is formed by interlacing two diagonal strips with a MASCLE *(q.v.)* (fig. 184, page 147). When the entire shield is covered with interlacing strips, the field is described as FRETTY (fig. 185, page 147).

FRETTY   See FRET

FRUCTED   When a plant is shown bearing fruit or seeds of a different tincture, the plant is said to be fructed of that tincture. Such fruit or seeds, to be visible at all, are always drawn in an outsized proportion (fig. 148, page 129).

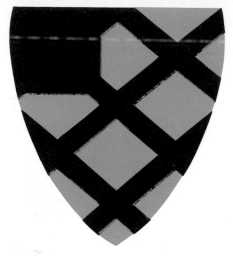

184   HARRINGTON   185   MIDDLETON

FUSILE   See LOZENGE

GARB   The heraldic term for a sheaf of grain (fig. 186).

186   MURPHY

GOLP   See ROUNDEL

GOUTTE (GOUTTÉ)   See SEMÉ

GRAND QUARTER   See QUARTER

GUARDANT   When a beast is represented with his body in profile but with his head turned forward to face the observer, the term guardant is added to the other terms of blazon to describe this variant position of the head. Thus the lions in fig. 187, are blazoned for position as PASSANT *(q.v.)* GUARDANT. When the head is completely turned so as to face the rear of an animal whose body is in profile, the term REGARDANT is used.

187   GRAGG

GULES   *See* TINCTURES

GYRON   The gyron is a triangular half of a QUARTER *(q.v.)*. It is formed by drawing a line from the center of the quartered shield (the fess point) to the opposite corner of the shield. A single gyron is a most unusual charge. Usually the field is composed entirely of gyrons of alternate metal and color; it is then blazoned GYRONNY (fig. 188). The term "gyronny," when used alone, is understood to mea n"gyronny of eight," each quarter being cut in half to produce two gyrons. If there are more or less in a particular coat-of-arms, the blazon should specify the number.

HAURIANT   A term often used instead of ERECT *(q.v.)* to describe a fish in the vertical position (fig. 146, page 128).

188   CAMPBELL

HELMET   In American usage the helmet is nothing more than a decorative adjunct to the complete ACHIEVEMENT *(q.v.)*. Elsewhere the helmet has considerable significance, indicating rank by tincture, position, and certain aspects of its visor. The closed helmet shown in profile and facing toward the dexter is indicative of the esquire or gentleman. This is the standard form in the United States, though certain variations are discussed in Chapter III, *Taking Your Coat-of-Arms Apart*.

As a decorative element, the helmet performs in addition the functional purposes of supporting the CREST *(q.v.)* and unifying the achievement by slightly overlapping the upper edge of the shield. And it provides a point of attachment for the MANTLING *(q.v.)* (fig. 69, page 51).

The helmet sometimes appears as a charge on the shield itself (fig. 189).

189   KENNEDY (2)

HERALDIC FURS   The divergent array of "furs" that appear in modern heraldry all stem from two real furs that were well known in the Middle Ages, *ermine* and *vair*.

ERMINE, a costly fur even then, was the more splendid of the two; it lined the cloaks of royalty and the great nobles. In time it came to be used as a covering for the entire shield or part of it. When armory passed from the actual carrying of shields to the graphic representation of them, this fur was depicted with reasonable accuracy by a white background bearing a number of small black tails. These tails were arranged for artistic purposes in a series of rows, a tail in any one row being between two tails in the row above or below it. The method of drawing the tails has undergone occasional change, but fig. 74, page 56 illustrates the standard modern way of representing this

149

fur. The "argent" background is nearly always shown as white, though in rare cases it is represented in silver.

Probably to satisfy the need for differencing arms of various branches of a given family using ermine, a new and purely heraldic fur was created called ERMINES. This merely reverses the colors of the natural fur; the background is black and the tails are white. In time, and again probably for the same reason, two other variants were created. ERMINOIS (fig. 74, page 56) has a gold background with black tails; the reverse is PEAN, which has a black field with golden tails.

The other basic fur, and one that came within the reach of anybody who could kill a few squirrels and prepare their hides, was VAIR. This was used extensively as a lining for cloaks, and eventually found its way onto the surface of shields. The best-known and prized variety of squirrel had a fur that was bluish-gray above and white below. Because the skin of the entire animal was used, the result (when several skins were conjoined) was a wavy sequence of alternating blotches of bluish-gray and white. Heraldic representation soon established symmetry. Although the symmetrical pattern has changed with the centuries, the present method of representing vair is in rows of shield-shaped figures alternately tinctured argent and azure (fig. 74, page 56). Out of this developed the variation known as COUNTER-VAIR, in which the odd numbered rows of "little shields" are shown upside down so that the long line of each "little shield" matches the long line of the "little shield" of the *same tincture* in the row beneath it (fig. 74, page 56). As in the case of ermine, the "argent" that is used in vair and counter-vair is generally shown as white rather than silver, though the latter is sometimes found. However, "vair" may be emblazoned in tinctures other than argent and azure. The usual variant is "or and gules" (gold and red); in which case it is customary not to use the term "vair," but to describe the fur as "VAIRY of or and gules."

In depicting the fur graphically it is a matter of small moment which comes first in the upper row, the metal or the color. However, general practice favors the metal.

Another geometrical variation of the original "vair" is the fur now known as POTENT. Here the alternating argent and azure portions of the squirrel skin are represented by rows of little "crutch heads," or *potents* (fig. 74, page 56). (*See also* CROSS POTENT.) These are so arranged that the head of any one "potent" never overlaps the head of another in the row above or below. If other than the standard tinctures are used, the fur is described as "POTENTY of (such tinctures)."

The variation of this fur is COUNTER-POTENT (fig. 74, page 56). Here the tinctures vary as in COUNTER-VAIR, forming vertical rows of color.

HERALDIC HEIRESS   A daughter whose arms-bearing father has no male heirs is termed a heraldic heiress. She and all sisters (through the paternal line) are considered "coheiresses."

HERALDS' TRICKS   See ENGRAVERS' TRICKS

HERALDRY   In the historic sense, the term heraldry includes the study of all the functions of a medieval herald. Among the primary services he performed for his lord were diplomatic missions in war and peace, arranging ceremonials, making formal announcements and proclamations, serving as a protocol officer, and, finally, maintaining genealogies and the regulation of coats-of-arms.

In modern times, heraldry is usually thought of as the science of coat armor and allied heraldic trappings. Many writers prefer the term armory as being of more specific application.

HILTED   When the hilt (including its crossbar and pommel) of the usual representation of a medieval sword is shown in a tincture that differs from that of the blade, it is described as hilted of that tincture (fig. 76, page 61).

HURT   See ROUNDEL

IMPALEMENT   A method of conjoining two separate coats-of-arms on a single shield. The shield is divided vertically down the center and a complete coat-of-arms is depicted on either side of the line of partition. It is the usual method of uniting the arms of husband and wife, showing the husband's arms on the dexter side and the wife's on the sinister (fig. 122a, page 101). It is used as well to join personal arms with arms of office, the official arms occupying the dexter half (fig. 124, page 114).

IN BEND   See BEND

IN CHEVRON   See CHEVRON

INCRESCENT   See CRESCENT

151

INESCUTCHEON   See ESCUTCHEON

IN FESS   See FESS

IN ORLO   See BORDURE

IN PALE   See PALE

IN PILE   See PILE

LABEL   The label is a small rakelike figure normally with three short tines. In English heraldry it is the cadence mark of the eldest son. The attached illustration (fig. 190) shows the simplest and most characteristic form of the label.

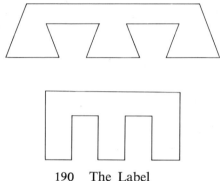

190   The Label

LANGED   When the tongue of an animal is shown of a separate tincture, the animal is described as langed of that tincture (fig. 35, page 34).

LILY   See FLEUR-DE-LYS

LIVERY COLORS   The dominant metal and color of a shield constitute the colors or livery colors of the arms. They are normally used as the tinctures of the TORSE (q.v.) or wreath and of the MANTLING (q.v.)

LODGED   See COUCHANT

LOZENGE   The lozenge in heraldry is a somewhat vertically lengthened diamond-shaped figure. It is often used in place of a shield in displaying the arms of a woman (fig. 191, page 152). It also occurs frequently as a charge (fig. 178, page 144). When the lozenge is pierced in the center with a circular opening, it is called a RUSTRE. When it is "voided," it becomes a MASCLE *(q.v.)*. When the entire shield or a specific area is covered with lozenges of alternating tinctures, that area is described as LOZENGY. The field in fig. 141, page 125 is described as "lozengy bendy." Fig. 192, shows a bend of lozenges.

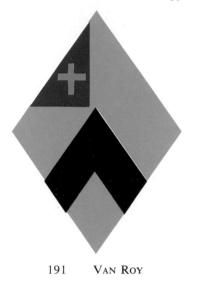

191   VAN ROY

192   RALEIGH (2)

The FUSIL, a narrower and more elongated figure, is a variation of the lozenge. Fig. 193, shows a fess of five fusils. Because its top and bottom angles are quite acute (French *aigu*), the fusil is used in the historic CANTING ARMS *(q.v.)* of the Montagus, where the family name is punned upon as *mont aigu,* "sharp-pointed mountain."

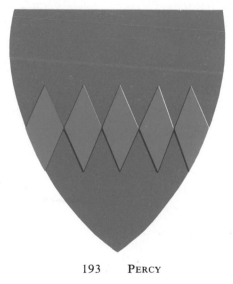

193   PERCY

LOZENGY   See LOZENGE

LUCY   An older name for the fish now known as the pike. It occurs as a charge in the canting arms of *Lucy* (fig. 146, page 128).

MANTLING   The mantling is an ornamental, cloaklike decoration depicted in an achievement of arms as depending from the upper portion of the helmet. In American usage it is always shown in the LIVERY COLORS *(q.v.);* the inner surface representing the dominant metal and the outer surface representing the dominant color. It is necessarily doubled over in places so as to show both surfaces (fig. 69, page 51).

MARSHALLING ARMS   A system of representing two or more distinct coats-of-arms on one shield. See IMPALEMENT, ESCUTCHEON OF PRETENCE, QUARTER, and Chapter V, " How Family Arms Grow."

MARTLET   The martlet is an essentially heraldic bird, always depicted without legs (fig. 194). In the English system of cadence marks, it is the symbol of the fourth son.

MASCLE   A mascle is a figure the size and shape of a lozenge, that is, a slightly elongated diamond, whose interior has been removed or VOIDED to leave only an outlining border (fig. 195).

194   MERIWETHER   195   BLAIR

MOON IN HER COMPLEMENT   See SUN IN HIS SPLENDOR

MOON IN HER DETRIMENT   See SUN IN HIS SPLENDOR

MOTTO   The motto, a short verbal expression associated with many but by no means all family coats-of-arms, is recorded on a narrow strip meant to suggest a SCROLL or RIBBON (fig. 69, page 51). When a motto is displayed as part of an achievement, American usage follows that of England; the scroll is placed below the shield. In the case of American arms of Scottish origin, the usage of that country is still generally adhered to; the motto surmounts the crest. The National Arms of the United States show a similar preference (fig. 123, page 112).

Moreover, Scottish usage makes a distinction between the motto, which may be any sort of an expression, and the more specialized CRI-DE-GUERRE, to which preferment is shown. The cri-de-guerre (war cry) has an unmistakable martial air about it. When it occurs in conjunction with a motto, it is customary to display the cri-de-guerre at the top of the achievement and the motto below.

MULLET   See STAR

MURREY   See TINCTURES

NAIANT   This term describes the horizontal or swimming position of a fish (fig. 196). Compare HAURIANT and EMBOWED.

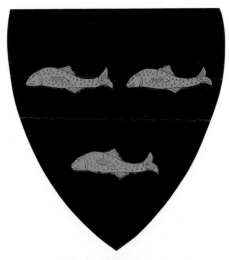

196   WELSH (WELCH)

NAVAL CROWN   See CORONETS

NOWED   This term is used in heraldry to describe anything that is tied into a knot. Fig. 80, page 68 shows "two serpents nowed vert in chief."

NOWY   A term used to describe one or more arches in an otherwise straight line. See the bottom leg of the isosceles triangle in fig. 197.

197   Schrader

OGRESS   See ROUNDEL

OR   See TINCTURES

ORDINARIES   See DIVISIONS OF THE SHIELD

ORLE   See BORDURE

OVAL   Any oval-shaped figure substituted for the more warlike shield in displaying arms. It is often used by clergymen to "pacify" their arms (fig. 125, page 115).

OVER ALL (SURTOUT)   A term used to indicate that a division of a shield is carried over one or more other divisions of a shield, partially obscuring the division(s) that it covers. In fig. 172, page 138, the bend sable is borne over all in relation to the quarterly divisions of the shield.

PADLOCK   See FETTERLOCK

PALE   A vertical stripe running through the central part of the shield (fig. 198, page 157). When charged it generally occupies about one-third of the shield, otherwise it may be somewhat reduced. The PALLET is a diminutive, one-half the width of the pale; it often occurs in pairs. A further diminutive is the ENDORSE, which is one-half the width of the PALLET; this is usually found in a group of three or more.

When a shield or one of its areas is divided into an even number of vertical stripes of alternate tinctures, it is said to be PALY of those tinctures. Even a charge may be PALY; (see fig. 199).

When several charges are arranged vertically in the central portion of the shield, they are said to be IN PALE (fig. 165, page 135).

When a shield or any area is divided vertically down the center to permit different tinctures on each side, it is PARTED PER PALE (fig. 200).

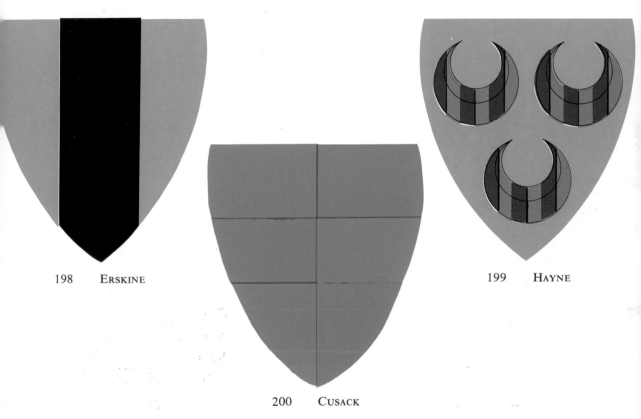

198   ERSKINE

200   CUSACK

199   HAYNE

PALL   The pall (more properly the ecclesiastical pallium worn by archbishops as a separate garment or embroidered on the chasuble of a celebrant) figures, as might be expected, in official church heraldry. When so used, it reproduces with reasonable faithfulness the article of clothing it represents. It is generally shown in silver or gold. It normally extends from the upper corners of the shield, as though hanging from the shoulders of the wearer, and ends at the base line with a deep fringe. When represented in this fashion, this Y-shaped figure partakes more of the nature of an *ordinary* (division of the shield) than of a *charge;* by many authorities it is considered one. It often carries charges on its surface as, in fact, the real pallium does.

Under the more commonplace name of SHAKEFORK, it appears in personal arms. It may then appear of any tincture and is usually couped, that is, it does not extend to the edges of the shield (fig. 201).

201   CUNNINGHAM

PALLET   See PALE

PALY   See PALE

PARTED PER BEND   See BEND

PARTED PER CHEVRON   See CHEVRON

PARTED PER FESS   See FESS

PARTED PER PALE   See PALE

PARTI-COLORED   Any object in heraldry is parti-colored if it is shown in more than one tincture. The division of tinctures, however, will normally follow an established heraldic pattern.

PARTITION LINES   Any line that divides the face of a shield into separate areas and tinctures is a partition line. Originally these lines were straight or smooth and followed the natural configuration of the division. In time they developed special or fanciful forms. The most frequently met partition lines are shown in the accompanying illustration (fig. 202).

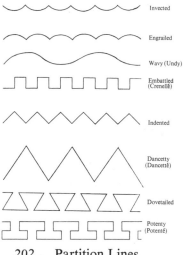

Invected

Engrailed

Wavy (Undy)

Embattled (Crenellé)

Indented

Dancetty (Dancetté)

Dovetailed

Potenty (Potenté)

202   Partition Lines

PASSANT   A term used to describe a four-footed animal in the act of walking. Unless otherwise specified, the animal is shown in profile (moving toward the dexter) with three feet on the ground and one foreleg elevated. The head is in profile and in line with the direction of the body (fig. 203). If the head is in any other position, the term that describes that position for the head must be added, such as in the term, "passant guardant" (fig. 187, page 148). See GUARDANT

203   JORDAN

PEAN   See HERALDIC FURS

PELICAN IN HER PIETY   The pelican, uniquely represented in the position known as "in her piety," is a direct borrowing from the pious symbolism of the medieval bestiaries. She is pictured as seated in her nest, surrounded by her young, and wounding her breast so as to feed them with her own blood (fig. 127, page 116). Shown argent on an azure field, this is the sole charge on the arms of the state of Louisiana.

PELLET   See ROUNDEL

PILE   This is a wedge-shaped figure and is always assumed to be "in chief" unless otherwise specified. When originating in chief, the base of this long triangle forms part of the top line of the shield and may stretch over as much as two-thirds of the top line. The point extends downward about three-quarters of the way toward the base of the shield. When two or more piles are placed together, each is necessarily made much smaller than a single pile would be. A pile may issue from any other line of the shield, but it must be described in the blazon as issuing from that particular place (fig. 204). The difficulty of a single pile in base is that, especially when a pointed shield is used, the result may be a shield that is divided per chevron. Usually, however, a single pile in base rises between two piles extending downward from the chief.

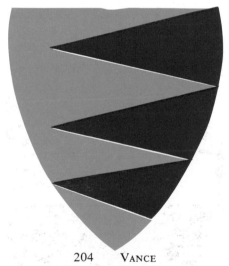

204   VANCE

Certain elongated charges, such as swords, darts, arrows, spears, or rods, when arranged in a triangular pattern with points meeting are said to be IN PILE.

PLATE   See ROUNDEL

160

PLATÉ (PLATY)   See SEMÉ

POMEY   See ROUNDEL

POMMELLED   When a sword or dagger is shown with its pommel (the round knob at the termination of the hilt) of a separate tincture, the blazon describes it as pommelled of that tincture (fig. 76, page 61).

POTENT(Y)   See HERALDIC FURS

PROPER   Describing a heraldic bearing as proper is a shorthand way of saying that the object is to be represented in its natural colors. But caution must be exercised in using this term when blazoning arms. An "oak tree proper" is not likely to be misunderstood; it will invariably be shown with a brown trunk and green foliage. But a "stallion proper" may readily become a horse of another color. When there are possible variations in coloration, it is much safer to specify the colors involved by their English names.

PURPURE   See TINCTURES

QUARTER   A quarter is one-fourth the face of the shield; it is produced by dividing the shield vertically through the center and then horizontally at the center. Each of the four resulting sections is a quarter (fig. 72, page 53). The first quarter, occupying the dexter chief, is the most important heraldically.

A distinction must be made between the quarter as a DIVISION OF THE SHIELD (q.v.) in a single or indivisible coat-of-arms (fig. 164, page 135) and the quarter as used in MARSHALLING ARMS, i.e., in representing several different coat-of-arms on one shield (fig. 122c, page 101). For in the latter case it is possible to have more than four quarters on a single shield. When this happens, the mathematical relationship is disregarded. As an example, if it were necessary to show five separate arms on a single shield, the so-called quarters would be drawn by dividing the upper half of the shield into three matching sections and the lower half into two. If six quarters were needed, the lower half would also be divided into three sections. If seven quarters were required, the upper half would consist of four sections and the lower of three. Notice that in marshalling multiple arms of an uneven number the upper half of the shield, being normally wider than the lower half, would carry the larger number. By the time you reach nine, it would be better to

161

have three rows instead of two. But each of these sections would still be called a quarter. A quarter that is itself "quartered" is called a GRAND QUARTER. Each of its smaller divisions is a SUBQUARTER.

205   HARLESTON

In modern armory the quarter as a division of a unit coat-of-arms normally appears fourfold. A single quarter is a rarity. What appears instead is the CANTON. This is, in a sense, the diminutive of the quarter. It ideally represents one-ninth of the shield, that is, the dexter third of the chief. Its actual size varies in modern usage. When it is a mere square of color, or even when it carries a single charge, it is frequently reduced in size. In Continental usage it is sometimes nearly as large as the quarter itself. Fig. 141, page 125 shows a "canton" as carried on a shield; the Dutch arms in fig. 191, page 153 show one as carried on a woman's LOZENGE *(q.v.)*.

QUATREFOIL   See CLOVERS

RAMPANT   This term describes the raging position of a major beast. The creature is shown in profile, normally facing toward the dexter. The body is reasonably erect; one hind leg touches the ground, the other three legs and the tail are elevated. The forelegs are in a conventional position of attack, indicated by the leg nearer the observer extended horizontally and the other foreleg raised beyond that roughly at a forty-five-degree angle. The head, with jaws open and teeth bared, is also assumed to be in profile and facing the dexter (fig. 206, page 163). If the head is in any other position, that position must be specified; see GUARDANT.

206   R EYNOLDS (1)

REGARDANT   See GUARDANT

RIBAND   See BEND

RIBBON   See MOTTO

ROACH (ROCHE)   The roach (Anglo-Norman *roche*) is, in America at least, an archaic name for a variety of carp. This fish is used as a pun on the family name in the arms of Roach, Roche (fig. 147, page 128). The same fish occur in the arms of Welsh, Welch (fig. 196, page 155).

ROSE   The heraldic rose is a stereotyped representation of the wild or single rose that was commonly known throughout the Middle Ages. (The double or semidouble garden variety of today is a cultivated variation of it.) Its conventionalized representation in heraldry shows the five distinct petals, between each two of which is seen the tip of a leaf. In the center are five or six small circles indicating the seeds. It may be of any tincture for heraldic purposes. When shown red, it is customary to color the leaf tips green and the seeds yellow or gold. It is then blazoned as "a rose gules, barbed *(q.v.)* vert and seeded or." "Barbed and seeded proper" would indicate the same treatment (fig. 138, page 123).

In some instances the rose is shown with a short stem to which two or three leaves are attached. It is then described as "slipped *(q.v.)* and leaved." If the stem and leaves are to be represented in a tincture different from that of the flower itself, that tincture must be specified; thus, "a rose gules, slipped and leaved vert."

In English heraldry the heraldic rose is the cadence mark of the seventh son.

ROUNDEL   A small, circular figure. It may be of any color, metal, or fur. It may be blazoned, accordingly, as a "roundel ermine," or a "roundel gules," etc. However, certain roundels have special names, so that neither the word roundel nor the specific tincture need be mentioned. The most usual of these are: *bezant*, gold; *golp*, purple; *hurt*, blue; *ogress* or *pellet*, black; *plate*, silver (fig. 151, page 129); *pomey*, green; and *torteau*, red. A very special type of roundel is the *fountain*. As the name implies, it is intended to represent a spring or pool; and it is always depicted as "barry wavy of six, argent and azure."

RUSTRE   See LOZENGE

SABLE   See TINCTURES

SALIENT   This term describes an animal in the act of leaping or springing forward. The animal is represented in profile, normally facing the dexter; the rear legs touch the ground; the body is erect, but inclined forward, and the forelegs are both elevated.

When two creatures are shown together in this position, they are normally depicted as leaping in opposite directions, one crossing the other, thus forming a saltire or X-shaped figure. They are then blazoned COUNTER-SALIENT.

SCRAPE   See BEND

SCROLL   See MOTTO

SEGREANT   A griffin in the rampant *(q.v.)* position is traditionally described as segreant.

SEJANT   This term describes a four-footed beast in the act of sitting. The basic and unmodified position is to represent the animal as seated on its haunches with the forelegs straight down and touching the ground. The creature is in profile and normally faces the dexter. If the head is not in profile with the rest of the body, its position must be specified. (See GUARDANT).

In some instances the animal, though seated on his haunches, is shown with body erect and forelegs raised in the position of a beast rampant. This position is glossed SEJANT-ERECT. Here again the head is assumed to be in profile; if not, its variant position must be specified. Thus, a beast depicted sitting on his haunches, body erect and forelegs elevated in the rampant posture, but with head turned to the rear, would be described as "sejant-erect regardant."

SEMÉ   The term semé (sown) indicates that the area described is powdered or strewn with an indefinite number of small figures. The repeated figure to be displayed is then specified. A shield blazoned "Gules, semé of crosses patté" means that the field is red and covered throughout by small crosses of the variety called "patté" (fig. 207). Note that these small crosses are not charges, but part of the field itself.

207   BERKELEY

Some stereotyped expressions have developed over the centuries to indicate that an area is semé of a particular symbol. Thus, the term VERDE is another way of saying "semé of leaves." CRUSILY means "semé of cross crosslets" (fig. 170, page 138); PLATY (or PLATE) is "semé of plates" (*i.e.,* silver roundels); BEZANTY (or BEZANTE), "semé of bezants" (*i.e.,* gold roundels). And BILLETTY means "semé of billets." In the term SEME-DE-LYS, the "lys" means "fleurs-de-lys." Similarly, GOUTE means "semé of gouttes (*i.e.,* drops)."

The GOUTTE (drop), a small pear-shaped figure, is a frequently used object for "powdering" a field. As this drop, or goutte, may be of any tincture, it is necessary to specify that tincture. Thus, a field may be described as "Argent, semé des gouttes gules" (fig. 208, page 166), which means that the silver shield is strewn with an indefinite number of small red drops. However, when gouttes are used for powdering, it is customary to describe the field as

165

goutté of the particular tincture. Thus, a blue shield strewn with golden colored drops is described, "Azure, goutté d'or."

208   TURNER

But a further nicety has been developed and is often used in blazon. Drops of certain colors have been given specific names. These are:

Argent (silver)	Goutté d'eau ("Droppy" of water)
Azure (blue)	Goutté de larmes (tears)
Gules (red)	Goutté de sang (blood)
Sable (black)	Goutté de poix (tar)
Vert (green)	Goutté de huile (oil)

Thus, the shield in fig. 208, may be blazoned in three ways: (a) *Argent, semé, des gouttes gules;* (b) *Argent, goutté de gules;* or (c) *Argent goutté de sang.* All are correct, but the last is the form most frequently used.

SHAKEFORK   See PALL

SHELLS   The two shells most frequently met with in armory are the ESCAL-LOP and the WHELK. The ESCALLOP (scallop shell) had the distinction of

209   GRAHAM

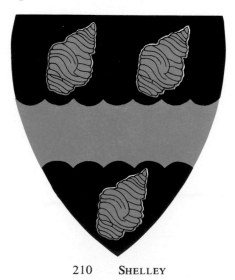

210   SHELLEY

serving as a badge of pilgrimage to the Holy Land, and its appearance in many arms may in fact commemorate such a pilgrimage (fig. 209, page 166). The WHELK, like the scallop, was an important food source in the coastal areas of medieval Europe. It occurs as a pun on the name in the canting arms of Shelley (fig. 210, page 166).

SHIELD   The shield or *escutcheon* in armorial representations is almost any configuration that vaguely suggests this defensive article of armor of the medieval warrior, and upon the surface of which the heraldic bearings are displayed. Modern usage prefers a shield of simple design.

SINISTER   The left side of the shield with reference to the man who is carrying the shield before him, therefore the right side from the viewpoint of the observer.

SLIPPED   When a leaf is shown with a small piece of the stem attached, it is customary to indicate this nicety by describing the leaf as slipped (fig. 211). This tiny piece of stem is always of the same tincture as the leaf itself. However, when a flower is described as slipped, the stem is shown of greater length and usually at least one leaf is attached to it. If more than one leaf is shown, the flower is generally described as "slipped and leaved." This addition to the flower may be of a different tincture, which is then specified; thus, "a rose gules, slipped and leaved vert."

211   HOLLINGSWORTH

SPUR-REVEL   See STAR

STAR (ESTOILE)   The unmodified term star is generally avoided in heraldry. Even when the conventional heraldic terms are used, the situation is confusing enough. The usual heraldic star is preferably called an ESTOILE; and, unless otherwise specified, it is assumed to be of six points or rays, each of which is drawn with wavy lines (fig. 212). Estoiles with a greater number of rays occur; the next most usual number being eight. When this matters, the number of rays should be specified. It is usual, but not obligatory, to depict the "estoile of eight rays" with the four rays that form an up-and-down cross drawn with straight lines and the four that form a saltire (diagonal cross) drawn with wavy lines. But this is an artistic nuance; all eight are frequently drawn with the characteristic wavy lines.

212   DRAKE

213   BRODIE

Our popular American conception of a star is the heraldic MULLET. This is the familiar star that appears in the arms of Washington (fig. 133, page 121), on the American flag, and in the crest of the Arms of the Republic (fig. 123, page 112). And in English heraldry it is the cadence mark of the third son. It is also known as the SCOTTISH STAR or the AMERICAN STAR. But, in origin, the MULLET (mollet) is the rowel of a spur, not a star at all (fig. 213). It is regularly depicted with five points formed by straight, not wavy, lines. Mullets of more than five points are used. When they are, the number of points must be specified; for technically these are not mullets at all, but rather straight-pointed stars. As such they will usually show six, sometimes eight, straight-edged points.

When the five-pointed mullet is pierced in the center by a circular opening, it is known as a SPUR-REVEL (fig. 214, page 169). The void or opening normally

168

shows the color of the field beneath the charge. On occasion, however, this opening is colored differently from the field beneath; in that case, it is necessary to describe the spur-revel as "pierced" of the new tincture.

214   MOULTRIE   215   THOMPSON

STATANT   When an animal is standing at rest with all four feet on the ground, it is described as statant.

SUB-QUARTER   See QUARTER

SUN IN HIS SPLENDOR   This term, with its variant, SUN IN ITS GLORY, is represented by a disc with rays extended from it in all directions (fig. 215). Though not obligatory, a human face is generally depicted on the disc. It is regularly and naturally tinctured "or" (gold).

A corresponding figure, without rays, represents the full moon and is blazoned the MOON IN IIER COMPLEMENT. It is usually shown in either silver or gold; its size and the figure of the human face distinguish it from a *bezant* or a *plate*. (See ROUNDEL.) On rare occasions it may be shown as black, and it is then glossed as the MOON IN HER DETRIMENT.

SUPPORTERS   A supporter is any figure—animal, human, even, in some instances, inanimate—placed beside a shield as though in the act of supporting it. They are nearly always used in pairs, one on either side of the shield; and the figure on one side need not be the same as that on the other. In some cases a shield is supported by a single figure standing beside it; but when one supporter is used, it is generally placed behind the shield, as in the Arms of the Republic (fig. 123, page 112).

As an almost invariable rule, supporters are an emblem of rank and authority. Where their use by individuals is concerned, they are associated with members of reigning families, members of the peerage (those individuals holding titles of nobility), and, in the British Isles, with members of certain specified orders of knighthood. Their use is limited to the individual holding such position, and it is not even extended to members of his immediate family. Accordingly, they have no place whatsoever in American family arms.

As symbols of authority, they may and do appear in the corporate arms of cities and states (fig. 216).

216   New Orleans, City of

SUPPORTERS FOR THE ARMS OF THE
CITY OF NEW ORLEANS

The unusual feature of these supporters is that they represent specific individuals. The dexter supporter is blazoned "Bienville" (*i.e.,* Jean Baptiste Le Moyne, Sieur de Bienville, founder of the City of New Orleans and French Governor of Louisiana); the other figure is identified as "Pere Marquette" (Father Jacques Marquette, French Jesuit missionary and early explorer of the Mississippi River).

SURTOUT   See OVER ALL

TENNÉ   See TINCTURES

217   CLAPP

TIERCED   A shield is said to be tierced or "parted per tierce" when it is divided horizontally into three equal parts (corresponding to chief, fess, and base) each of a separate tincture (fig. 217).

TINCTURES   Historically and technically, the term tincture may apply to anything that provides a covering in color to the surface of a shield or to its charges. In this sense it would include not only the heraldic colors and metals but also the HERALDIC FURS *(q.v.)*. Because of the basic difference in nature between furs and colors, modern usage prefers to consider them separately, and they are so treated here.

The only heraldic metals are *argent* (white or silver) and *or* (yellow or gold); the most usual colors are: *azure* (blue), *gules* (red), *vert* (green), *purpose* (purple), and *sable* (black). The engravers' tricks by which these metals and colors are represented in monochrome renderings are illustrated in fig. 74, page 56.

Two rather unusual colors are *tenné* (tawny orange) and *murrey* (maroon). Tenné is represented in the engravers' tricks with vertical lines cross-hatched by diagonal lines running in the direction of a bend sinister. Murrey is represented by cross-hatching diagonal lines running in opposite directions, that is, one set in the direction of the bend dexter and the other set in the direction of the bend sinister.

TORSE   The torse or WREATH is a stylized ornament that follows the contour of the upper part of the helmet and out of which the crest rises (fig. 69, page 51). In some achievements it is replaced by a CORONET *(q.v.)*. American usage closely follows that of Britain; the torse is shown in six segments, representing two twisted pieces of cloth. These segments alternate in presenting the LIVERY COLORS *(q.v.)*, that is, the dominant metal and color of the arms in that order.

Continental usage is considerably freer in depicting the torse. Often, especially in German armory, an odd number of segments is shown (usually five or seven), in which case the color comes first and last. In some instances two colors and a metal are used, often conveying a more representative picture of the armorial tinctures.

When, in an abbreviated achievement, the helmet is omitted, the crest torse is usually represented by a straight bar of six segments (fig. 73, page 55).

TORTEAU   See ROUNDEL

TREFOIL   See CLOVERS

TRESSURE   See BORDUE

TRICKING   See ENGRAVERS' TRICKS

TRIPPANT   The term trippant is used to describe the walking motion of a member of the deer family. The animal is shown in profile (normally facing the dexter) with three legs on the ground. One foreleg is elevated and bent downward from the knee (fig. 132, page 121). It is roughly equivalent to the term "passant" *(q.v.)* as applied to other four-footed animals.

VAIR(Y)   See HERALDIC FURS

VERDE   See SEME

VERT   See TINCTURES

VOIDED   This term voided is used to describe a figure whose interior portion has been removed or voided, so as to leave merely a narrow border. Thus, the MASCLE, *(q.v.),* is merely a lozenge voided (fig. 195, page 154).

VORANT   The term vorant is used to describe a creature in the act of devouring another (fig. 218).

218   VISCONTI

172

VULNED   When a creature is depicted as wounded, it is blazoned as vulned, and the location of the wound is specified. In the representation, the wound is indicated by drops of blood.

WHELK   See SHELLS

-WISE (-WAYS)   This suffix is used in some blazons to mean "in the manner of" the term to which it is attached. Thus, if several small charges are arranged diagonally from dexter chief to sinister base, they are sometimes described as *bendwise* or *bendways*. The term is equivalent here to *in bend*. Similarly, *fesswise* means *in fess, saltirewise* means *in saltire*, etc. It is more often used, however, to describe the position of a single charge; thus "a lance bendwise sinister" would describe this weapon placed in the direction of a bend sinister.

WREATH   See TORSE

A Selected Bibliography

The following references have been selected for three reasons: (a) they meet the needs of the beginning student of heraldry; (b) they are in English; and (c) they are readily available. And each of them contains a brief or fairly extensive bibliography for further study. (Missing from the list are the old stand-bys, Burke, Debrett, and Fairbairn.)

If you have a special interest in the heraldic or genealogical studies of non-English speaking countries, Constance M. Winchell's *Guide to Reference Books* (7th Edition, 1951) with its supplements (1953-1955; 1956-1958) is the basic bibliographical tool. Look under such headings as "Genealogy," "Heraldry," "Names," "Orders and Decorations," and "Titles."

Good luck and pleasant hours!

Encyclopaedia Britannica. The article on "Heraldry" by Oswald Barron is a basic introduction to the science. It is reprinted in all recent editions, but if you are fortunate enough to have available the now-classic Eleventh Edition (1910-1911), consult it. In addition to the four full-color plates of historic arms, the many black-and-white illustrations are completely blazoned.

Fox-Davies, A. C., *Complete Guide to Heraldry*. Edinburgh, London, New York, 1901; Thomas Nelson & Sons, Ltd., reprinted 1956.

This is the most comprehensive and rewarding study of British heraldry in modern times. Every aspect of heraldic usage is covered in complete detail.

Grant, Francis J., *Manual of Heraldry*. Edinburgh, John Grant, 1937.

An excellent manual of general heraldry with special attention to usage in Scotland.

Hope, W. H. St. John, *Heraldry for Craftsmen and Designers*. New York, 1913. The Macmillan Company.

A storehouse of valuable information for the professional craftsman.

Moncreiffe, Iain, and Pottinger, Don, *Simple Heraldry*. Edinburgh, London, New York. Thomas Nelson & Sons, Ltd., reprinted 1957.

By far the most effective simple introduction for anyone, it has become both a "must" and a delight for children.

Wagner, Anthony, *Heraldry in England*. Penguin Books, Inc., Baltimore, Md., reprinted 1951.

Rich in color and good sense, here are "infinite riches in a little room."

Doan, Gilbert H., *Searching for Your Ancestors*. The University of Minnesota Press, Minneapolis, Minn., revised edition 1948.

INDEX OF BLAZONS

The following verbal descriptions represent several styles of blazoning. This results, in a few instances, from specific requests that I use blazons as preserved in family papers or recorded in published family histories. Unusual forms of family names are in response to similar requests. In most cases, however, I have deliberately varied the style of the blazons so that the beginning student may become familiar with an acceptable range of variations.

AHERNE (1) (AHEARNE)—Vert, three herons argent.

AHERNE (2)—Per fess argent and azure, three chaplets, two in chief, one in base, counterchanged.

ANDERSON—Or, on a chevron gules between three eagles' heads erased sable, as many acorns slipped argent.

BARNWELL—Ermine, a bordure engrailed gules.

BARRETT—Barry of ten per pale argent and gules counterchanged.

BARRY—Argent, three bars gemels gules.

BECK (1)—Gules, a cross moline argent.

BECK (2)—Argent, on a fess indented azure, between (in chief) two cocks' heads erased gules and (in base) a blackbird sable, an annulet between two crosses potent or.

BERKELEY—Gules, semé of crosses patté argent, a chevron of the second.

BLAIR—Argent, on a saltire sable nine mascles of the field.

BLAKE (1)—Argent, a chevron between three garbs sable.

BLAKE (2)—Argent, a fret gules.

BOYD—Azure, a fess checky or and gules.

BRIGGS—Gules, three bars gemels or, a canton sable.

BRINDLEY—Parted per pale or and sable, a chevron countercolored between three escallops countercolored.

BRISBANE—Sable, a chevron checky or and gules between three wool packs of the second.

BRISCOE—Argent, three greyhounds courant sable in pale.

BRODIE—Argent, a chevron gules between three mullets azure.

BRUCE—Or, a saltire gules, a chief of the second.

BRYANT, THE REVEREND JAMES C., JR.—Azure, on a cross or a cinquefoil between four lozenges gules; all on an oval within a belt gray, fringed sable, buckled of the second, and surmounted by a clerical hat with two tassels of the fifth.

BUCK—Lozengy bendy of eight or and azure, a canton ermine.

BULL—Gules, an armored arm bearing a sword argent.

BURKE—Or, a cross gules.

BURNS—Or, a fess between (in chief) three spur-revels and (in base) a hunting horn, all sable.

BUTLER—Gules, three covered cups or.

BYRON—Argent, three bendlets sinister in chief gules. (A variant blazon would be: Argent, three scrapes enhanced gules.)

CAMERON—Gules, three bars or.

CAMPBELL—Gyronny of eight or and sable.

CARROLL—Argent, two lions erect aspectant gules supporting a sword proper.

CARROLL, THE MOST REVEREND COLEMAN F., Bishop of Miami—Impaled arms. Dexter. Azure, a fess abased or, issuant therefrom a palm tree of the same between two Latin crosses patté argent, in base four bars wavy of the last (Diocese of Miami). Sinister. Per chevron argent and gules, two lions rampant affrontée counterchanged supporting a processional cross patté or, in base two martlets affrontée of the first (Bishop Carroll). Behind the shield a processional cross between a mitre and a crosier, all or; the whole ensigned with a pontifical hat bearing six tassels on either side vert. Motto: Primum Regnum Dei.

CHAMBERLAIN—Gules, a fess between three escallops or.

CHAUCER—Parted per pale argent and gules, a bend counterchanged.

CHISHOLM—Gules, a boar's head couped or.

CLAPP—Parted per tierce vair, argent, and gules.

CLARK—Gules, a cross argent.

CLAY—Argent, a chevron engrailed between three trefoils slipped sable.

CLERY—Or, three nettle leaves vert.

CLOPTON—Sable, a bend argent between two cotises dancetté or.

COFFEY (COFFEE)—Vert, three covered cups or.

COFFIN OF NANTUCKET—Azure, five cross-crosslets in saltire or between four bezants.

COLLETON—Or, three stags' heads couped proper.

COLLINS—Argent, two lions rampant combatant proper.

COLONNA—Gules, a column argent, base and capital or.

CONNOLLY—Argent, on a saltire sable five escallops of the field.

CORBETT—Or, three corbets sable.

COSTELLO—Or, three fusïls azure.

CRAWFORD—Gules, a fess ermine.

CROSLAND (CROSSLAND)—Quarterly argent and gules, a cross fleury counter-changed.

CUMMINGS (CUMMINS)—Purpure, three garbs or.

CUNNINGHAM—Argent, a shakefork sable.

CUSACK—Parted per pale or and azure, a fess counterchanged.

DACRE—Gules, three scallop shells argent.

DAVENPORT—Argent, a chevron between three cross-crosslets fitchy sable.

DAVIS OF CAROLINA—Azure, a fess or between three mullets of six points argent.

DEVEREUX—Gules, a fess argent, three plates in chief.

DOUGLAS—Argent, a heart gules regally crowned or, on a chief azure three mullets of the first.

DOWD—Vert, a saltire or.

DRAKE—Sable, a fess wavy between two estoiles argent.

DRUMMOND—Or, three bars wavy gules.

DUNDAS—Argent, a lion rampant gules.

ELLIOT—Gules, a bend engrailed or.

ERSKINE—Argent, a pale sable.

FERGUSON—Azure, three boars' heads couped or.

FITZGERALD—Argent, a saltire gules.

FITZPATRICK—Sable, a saltire argent.

FLEMING (FLEMMING)—Vair, a chief checky gules and or.

FORBES—Azure, three boars' heads erased argent, langed and muzzled gules.

FRENCH—Ermine, a chevron sable.

GIBBS—Quarterly. 1 and 4, argent, three axcs sable; 2 and 3, argent, two lozenges in fess gules.

GILFOIL (GILFOYLE)—Azure, two bars argent.

GILLENTINE—Azure, a fess or between three swans proper.

GRADY—Parted per pale gules and sable, three lions passant in pale parted per pale argent and or.

GRAGG—Argent, three lions passant guardant in pale azure.

GRAHAM—Or, on a chief sable three escallops of the field.

GRANT—Gules, three antique crowns or.

GREBY—Ermine, two flanches azure, each bearing three ears of wheat or.

HAHN—Sable, three gamecocks or.

HALLIDAY—Sable, three helmets argent, garnished or, a bordure engrailed of the second.

HAMILTON—Gules, three cinquefoils argent.

HANNON—Quarterly gules and or, on a bend sable three crosses patté argent.

HARLESTON—Quarterly. 1 and 4, argent, a fess ermine cotised sable (for Harleston); 2 and 3, sable, a chevron between three leopards' heads or (for Wentworth).

HARRINGTON—Sable, a fret argent.

HATFIELD—Ermine, on a chevron sable three cinquefoils argent.

HAWLEY—Vert, a saltire invected argent.

HAY—Argent, three inescutcheons gules.

HAYNE—Argent, three crescents paly of six gules and azure.

HERIOT—Argent, on a fess azure three cinquefoils of the first.

HEYWARD—Azure, a chevron per pale or and ermine between three garbs of the second.

HILLIS—Parted per pale or and gules, a lion passant guardant proper.

HOLBROOK—Argent, crusily sable, a chevron gules.

HOLLINGSWORTH—Azure, on a bend argent three holly leaves slipped vert.

HOME—Vert, a lion rampant argent.

HOMER—Argent, a crossbow unbent sable between four gamecocks gules.

HORNER—Sable, three talbots proper.

HOUSTON OF GEORGIA—Or, a chevron checky sable and argent between three martlets of the second.

HOWARD—Gules, a bend between six cross-crosslets fitchy argent.

HUTSON—Per chevron embattled or and vert, three martlets counterchanged.

HYNES—Parted per pale or and gules, two lions rampant combatant countercolored.

INNES—Argent, in chief three mullets azure.

IZARD—Argent, six leopards' faces vert, three, two, and one.

JORDAN—Argent, a fess sable, in base a lion passant of the second.

KENNEDY (1)—Argent, a chevron gules between three cross-crosslets fitchy sable.

KENNEDY (2)—Sable, three helmets in profile proper.

KERR—Gules, on a chevron argent three mullets of the field.

KLAVENESS, F. A.—Azure, on a cloven ness extending from two mountains a castle, all argent.

LACY—Or, a lion rampant purpure.

LATIMER—Gules, a cross fleury or.

LAUNCELOT, SIR—Gules, a griffin segreant or.

LEE OF VIRGINIA—Azure, a fess checky gules and argent between eight brillets or.

LINDSAY—Gules, a fess checky argent and azure.

LIPPE—Argent, a rose gules barbed and seeded proper.

LOCKHART—Argent, a heart gules within a padlock sable.

LORING—Quarterly argent and gules, a bend engrailed of the second.

LOWY—Per bend argent and gules, on a bend sable a lion passant or.

LUCY—Gules, three lucies hauriant or.

LYNCH—Azure, a chevron between three trefoils or.

MACDONOGH (MACDONOUGH) (MCDONOGH)—Parted per chevron invected or and vert, in chief two lions guardant gules, in base a boar passant argent.

MACEWAN—Parted per fess purpure and or, in chief a lion passant argent, in base a garb of the first.

MACFARLANE (MCFARLAN)—Argent, a saltire wavy between four cinquefoils gules.

MACKENZIE—Azure, a stag's head caboshed or.

MACLENNAN (LOGAN)—Or, a heart gules pierced by a broad-arrow proper.

MALCOLM (MACCALLUM)—Argent, on a saltire azure between four stags' heads erased gules, five mullets of the first.

MANNERS—Or, two bars azure, a chief gules.

MANNING (1)—Quarterly azure and gules, a cross fleury between four trefoils argent.

MANNING (2)—Vert, a chevron between three trefoils or.

MARTIN—Ermine, three bars gules.

MATHESON—Argent, three dexter hands couped at the wrist gules.

MCARTHUR—Azure, a cross moline argent between three antique crowns or.

MCCARTHY—Argent, a stag trippant gules, attired and unguled or.

MEEHAN (MEIGHAN)—Gules, on a chevron argent three bucks' heads erased of the first, attired or.

MENZIES—Argent, a chief gules.

MERIWETHER—Or, three martlets sable, on a chief of the second a sun in his glory.

MIDDLETON—Argent, fretty sable, a canton of the second.

MORGAN—Or, a griffin segreant sable.

MOULTRIE—Azure, on a chevron between three escallops argent, a boar's head couped sable and two spur-revels gules.

MUNRO (MONROE) (MONRO)—Or, an eagle's head erased gules.

MURPHY—Quarterly argent and gules, on a fess sable between four lions rampant countercolored, three garbs or.

NOBLE—Argent, three bay leaves slipped vert.

NOBLE, JOHN T.—Parter per chevron argent and vert, three bay leaves counterchanged. Crest: on a torse of the colors a bay tree proper. Motto: Virtute et Valore.

NUGENT—Ermine, two bars gules.

O'DAY—Argent, in base a hand proper cuffed azure, holding a sword erect, blade of the third, hilted or; in chief two serpents nowed vert.

O'TOOLE—Gules, a lion passant argent.

PERCY—Azure, a fess fusily of five or.

PLOWDEN—Azure, a fess dancetty, the three upper points terminating in fleurs-de-lys or.

POLLÀTSEK-PORTOS—Quarterly sable and gules, a leaf argent. Crest: A demi-lion rampant quarterly sable and gules, langed of the second, armed argent, and charged with a leaf of the last.

POWER—Argent, a chief indented sable.

PRATT—Argent, on a fess between three elephants' heads erased sable, as many mullets of the field.

PRICE—Gules, a lion rampant argent.

RALEIGH (1)—Vert, two lions erect aspectant or, supporting a dexter hand couped gules.

RALEIGH (2) (RALEGH)—Gules, a band indented argent.

READE (READ)—Azure guttée d'or, a cross-crosslet fitchée of the second.

REYNOLDS (1) Vert, a lion rampant between three escallops or.

REYNOLDS (2)—Azure, a chevron checky or and gules between three cross-crosslets fitchy of the second.

REYNOLDS, SHERMAN BRIGGS II—Quarterly; 1 and 4, azure, three foxes statant in pale argent (for Reynolds); 2 and 3, parted per chevron argent and vert, three bay leaves countercharged (for Noble). Crest, a fox statant argent. Motto: Virtute et Valore.

RHETT—Or, a cross engrailed sable.

ROACH (ROCHE)—Gules, three roches naiant in pale argent.

RUST OF VIRGINIA—Argent, a cross saltire azure between (in chief and base) two battle axes and (in dexter and sinister) two crosses patté fitché gules.

SCHRADER—Argent, an isosceles triangle, bottom leg nowy, with plumb-bob pendant gules.

SCOTT—Or, on a bend azure an estoile between two crescents argent.

SEABROOK—Argent, a cross gules, in dexter chief a cross-crosslet fitchy sable.

SETON (SEATON)—Or, three crescents gules.

SHAKESPEARE—Or, on a bend sable a tilting spear of the field.

SHELLEY—Sable, a fess engrailed between three whelk shells or.

SHERMAN—Or, a lion rampant sable between three oak leaves vert.

SIMONS OF SOUTH CAROLINA—Parted per chevron embattled gules and sable, three martlets argent.

SNOOKS (1) (SENNOKS)—Or, an oak tree eradicated proper, fructed with seven of the first.

SNOOKS (2)—Vert, seven acorns or.

STACKHOUSE—Argent, three saltires couped gules in chevron between (in chief) a stackhouse proper and (in base) a garb vert.

STAFFORD—Or, a chevron gules.

STANDISH—Sable, three plates. (The plates or roundels argent are frequently blazoned as "standishes" or "standing dishes.")

STANFORD—Vert, on a bend wavy three plates.

STOKES OF GEORGIA—Sable, a lion rampant ermine.

SULLIVAN—Argent, in base a hand couped and erect gules, clutching a sword azure, hilted and pommeled or.

SUTHERLAND—Gules, three mullets argent.

THOMPSON—Or, on a fess dancetté azure three estoiles argent; on a canton of the second the sun in glory proper.

TIERNEY—Argent, a chevron sable, a chief gules.

TOBIN—Azure, three oak leaves argent.

TOMKINS (TOMPKINS)—Azure, on a chevron between three moorcocks close or, as many cross-crosslets sable.

TORRENCE (TORRANCE)—Parted per pale gules and or, two boat's oars in saltire azure.

TRAVIS—Sable, a chevron between (in chief) two escallops and (in base) a boar's head erased, all argent.

TULLY—Vert, a chevron between three wolves' heads erased argent.

TURNER—Argent, goutté de sang, a wheel sable.

URQUHART—Or, three boars' heads couped gules.

VANCE—Argent, three piles issuant in sinister gules.

VAN ROY (VAN ANROOY)—Argent, a chevron sable, on a canton gules a cross or.

VISCONTI—Argent, a serpent azure, crowned or, vorant a child proper.

WALLER—Sable, three walnut leaves or in bend between two cotises argent.

WALSH—Argent, a chevron gules between three broadarrow heads points upward sable.

WASHINGTON—Argent, two bars gules, in chief three mullets of the second.

WAYNE—Gules, a chevron ermine between three gauntlets or.

WELSH (WELCH)—Sable, three fish naiant argent.

WILLARD—Argent, on a chevron sable between three fish weels proper, five ermine spots of the first. (The weels are sometimes blazoned "villerdes"; this Old French term for the "weel" or fish trap provides a canting reference to the name. Another blazon might be: Argent, a chevron ermines between three villerdes proper. In some modern versions of these arms, the fish weel is replaced by a "flask" or "jar.")

WILLSON—Or, a wolf rampant between three inescutcheons sable, on each inescutcheon a leaf of the first.

WOODWARD—Azure, a pale between two eagles displayed argent.

WOOLRIDGE—Argent, a cross quarterpierced sable between four crescents gules.

WRAGG—Or, a fess azure, on a canton of the second a fleur-de-lys of the first.

WRIGHT (1)—Argent, on a pale gules between two crosses moline azure, an eagle displayed sable.

WRIGHT (2)—Azure, two bars argent, in chief three leopards' faces or.

YEAMANS (1)—Sable, a chevron between three spear heads argent.

YEAMANS (2)—Sable, a chevron between three cronels argent.

ZAMORANO Y GONZALES—Impaled arms. Dexter. Gules, a tower argent, on a bordure or eight torteaux (for Zamorano). Sinister. Quarterly; 1 and 4, or, a lion salient proper; 2 and 3, gules, a saltire couped or (for Gonzales).